The Narrow Winding Road
Shave Ice Solomon

THERE ARE MANY WAYS TO RELATE TO THE HANA HIGHWAY:

A ROAD CONNECTING TWO POINTS,

A SCENIC DELIGHT, A METAPHOR OF LIFE.

FOR SOME PEOPLE THE HANA HIGHWAY IS ART.

(1) The Road Narrows Sign heavily coated with jungle mold.

THE NARROW WINDING ROAD
by Shave Ice Solomon

Copyright 1994 - T ~ N Productions
In association with Barton Jay Productions

ISBN: 0-9626070-2-9
Library of Congress Number: 93-85867

ALL RIGHTS RESERVED
No material in this book may be copied,
reproduced or used in any way without express
written permission of the author or publisher
except for portions thereof reprinted in critical reviews.

TO ORDER ADDITIONAL COPIES OF THIS BOOK
Send a check or M.O. for the cover price, $8.95 plus $1.05 (S&H) and
make payable to:
T ~ N
P. O. Box 841
Hana, Maui, Hawai'i 96713

ACKNOWLEDGEMENTS
Thanks to the many friends who assisted
in editing text, culling photographs, designing,
producing & marketing.

TEXT & PHOTOGRAPHY BY SHAVE ICE SOLOMON
All pictures were taken with an Olympus Infinity Twin Auto Focus 35mm
Camera with a 70mm telephoto adjustment.

TYPESETTING & LAYOUT BY SHAVE ICE SOLOMON
All production work was done on a Macintosh SE using Pagemaker 4.0.

THIS BOOK IS HOME GROWN.
Printed in the United States of America

HANA CASSETTE GUIDE
Your personal guide to paradise

You pick up the **Hana Cassette Guide** package in the morning on your way to Hana. Your package includes a tape player, flower and tree identification photo book and a souvenir Hana Coast map. It's just like having your own personal tour guide sitting on the seat next to you. This is a fully-coordinated narrated tour as the narrator, Craig, has you turn the tape player on and off all along the way. You'll hear about the history, legends, plants and flowers as you discover the waterfalls, hidden pools and black sand beaches of Maui's famous Hana Highway.

We highly recommend this informative and interesting guide to anyone planning a leisurely drive to Hana and the 'Ohe'o/Seven Pools area of Maui. Since 1985 the **Hana Cassette Guide** has been providing this popular audio cassette tour of Maui's famous Hana Highway.

Hana Cassette Guide is located at the Shell service station in Kahului on Route 380, just before you make the right hand turn onto the Hana Highway (Route 36).

Table Of Contents

BEFORE WE BEGIN	5
BEGINNING AT THE BEGINNING	6
THE ROAD TO HANA	12
DRIVING THE HANA HIGHWAY	20
SIGNS OF THE HANA HIGHWAY	26
HA - TO BREATHE OR NOT TO BREATHE	30
ORIGIN OF MAUI & THE HAWAIIAN ISLANDS	38
HALF WAY TO HANA & UNCLE HARRY'S	44
ISLAND POLITICS	48
BAMBOO	56
THE COCONUT PALM TREE	59
LOWER NA-HIKU ROAD	60
LIFE IN HANA	68
HANA MEDICAL CENTER	78
HASEGAWA'S GENERAL STORE	81
'OHE'O GULCH & THE SEVEN POOLS	90
KI-PAHULU	98
LEAVING HANA SIDE	102
CHANGES SINCE I BEGAN THIS BOOK	103
BIBLIOGRAPHY	104

Shave Ice Solomon's Reviews

HANA: WHERE TO STAY & WHAT TO DO	108
PA'IA: OUR FAVORITE PLACES	112
KA-HULUI: BACK TO THE BEGINNING	118
OTHER WONDERFUL MAUI THINGS TO DO	120

(2) Cocos nuciferas - The Coconut Palm Tree

(3) The ocean breaking against lava rocks off Na-hiku Point.

(4) Many, many, many One Lane Bridges - Ku-pu-koi Bridge, after Mile Marker #25.

(5) The jungle hangs over the Hana Highway and the Road disappears around many corners.

(6) Just another Road Side Attraction - Pu-oho-ka-moa Falls, Mile Marker #11.

BEFORE WE BEGIN

I love the Road to Hana. I have driven it more times than I can count. My purpose in writing this book was to capture my love of the Hana Highway experience in the flood of images that confront visitor and resident alike.

As your Guide, I will show you the sparkling waterfalls, coastline panoramas and outstanding points of interest along with the other road side attractions. Around each curve of the Road you will find something different. There are the narrow roads and bridges, the innumerable twists and turns, the large trucks coming at you, and even the road crew filling the constantly reappearing potholes.

I have also included personal vignettes along with insights into island history, politics and environmental issues. It has been my intention to give the outsider a glimpse of Hana life and of island life from a perspective few who do not live here could possibly find anywhere else. I also wanted to record my memories of a time and place.

The last section of the book includes a special directory of places to stay and things to do in Hana. The book ends with reviews of the best things to do and my favorite places to eat on Maui.

(7) A Wiggle Ahead Sign.

I am sure you will enjoy reading my book as much as I enjoyed writing it. I know you will also find it a wonderful way of remembering your own experience of **The Narrow Winding Road.**

(8) The Road wiggles just like the signs.

BEGINNING AT THE BEGINNING

Officially, the Hana Highway extends from Ka-hu-lui, where it elbows into stately Ka'ahu-manu Boulevard, past Baldwin Beach Park and the sugar cane/tourist town of Pa'ia. Next comes Ku'au, home of Mama's Fish House and Ho'okipa Beach.

(9) Windsurfing Capital of the World

Ho'okipa Beach is called the Windsurfing Capital of the World as the trade winds blow along the coast here at wave jumping speed. Ho'okipa is the Hawaiian word for 'hospitality.'

After Ho'okipa you drive through the pineapple fields of Ha'i-ku and through the countryside of Huelo with its wind swept hills where people live snugly in valleys invisible from the Hana Highway.

As you pass through Huelo, you enter into the thick rainforest where, due to the heavier rains, the jungle becomes more intense.

It is also after Huelo that the Hana Highway becomes a narrow road twisting and turning along the coast past many waterfalls, over narrow one lane bridges, past beautiful Wai-lua & Ke-'anae Peninsulas, through the even wetter rainforest of Na-hiku and on through Hana town out to 'Ohe'o Gulch.

After 'Ohe'o Gulch, the paved road ends as you drive through Ki-pahulu to the dirt road called the Old King Pi'i-lani Highway. This section of the road is more commonly referred to as the Kau-po Road. It is the last remaining section of the original road constructed by an early Maui chief, Kepa-a-Pi'i-lani who ruled around 1300 AD.

The first ten miles of the Old King Pi'i-lani Highway are indicated on the tourist maps as an impassable, unpaved road, stating: "drive at your own risk."

And risky it is. The rent-a-car companies waver responsibility for lost mufflers, scratched and ruined paint and whatever else can happen when you are two hours away from civilization on an unpaved back road.

Part of the Kau-po Road is graded while other parts are somewhat leveled rocks, barely cut into the side of the cliff above a constantly crashing ocean.

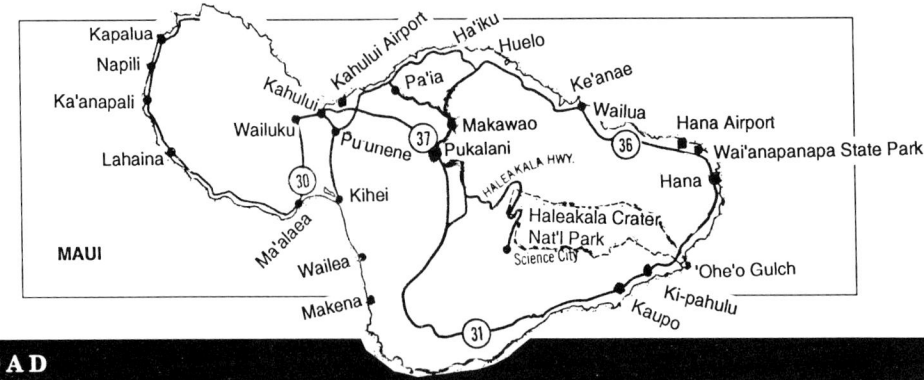

(10) "The Hana Highway...elbows into stately Ka'ahumanu Boulevard...." - 55 miles to Hana.

(11) Rush hour where Dairy Road, coming from the Ka-hu-lui Airport, intersects with the Hana Highway - 54 miles to Hana.

(12) Crossing the isthmus of central Maui headed toward the Hale-a-kala Highway intersection.

(13) Hale-a-kala, a 10,023 ft. volcano, dominates the landscape. To get to Hana you have to go around to the other side of this mountain.

(14) Baldwin Park is not a tourist beach; it is an unassuming family beach without hotels or condominiums.

(15) Locals park their vehicles at the beach to talk story, listen to car stereos and to watch the bikinis and waves.

(16) Everyday is children's day at Baldwin Beach Park.

(17) Even with clouds heavy in the sky, Baldwin Beach is filled with people playing in the surf.

(18) *The first stop as you enter Pa'ia is the Maui Crafts Guild co-operatively owned and operated by 40 outstanding local craftspeople.*

(19) *No matter how wet the rest of the Hana coast gets, it is almost a guarantee that the sun will be shining in Pa'ia. Only 30" of rain a year.*

(20) *Once a busy plantation town, now the streets of Pa'ia are lined with boutiques, eateries and art galleries.*

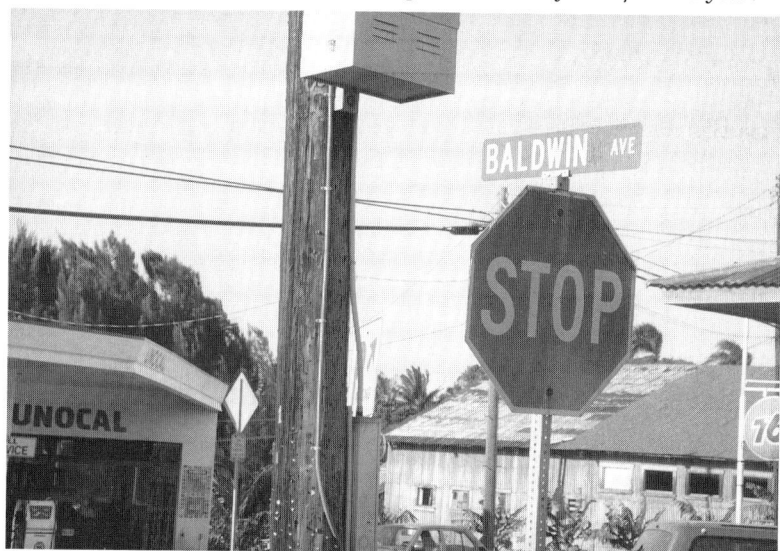

(21) *A reminder of the past, the Stop Sign where Baldwin Ave. meets the Hana Highway. The Stop Sign has now been replaced by a traffic light.*

(22) The old Kuau Store is now painted white with a pinkish stripe emblazoned with the words: KUAU PIT STOP.

(23) Mama's Fish House is the place to enjoy an outstanding sunset along with fine wine and food. Eating at Mama's is an island tradition.

(24) Ho'okipa Beach Park looking back to Ka-hu-lui and Wai-lu-ku nestled at the foot of heavily eroded Eke Crater (the West Maui Mts.).

(25) Windsurfers from around the world gliding along at Ho'okipa Beach looking for waves to jump.

(26) Landscape is pretty flat between Pa'ia and the beginning of the Hana Highway Coastal Road.

(27) A local chicken waits patiently to cross the Hana Highway.

(28) Maui Grown Market (past Mile Marker #14) is a great place to stop for sandwiches, snacks, cold drinks, produce and many gift items.

(29) The jungle pools at Ho'olawa Bridge, locally known as Twin Falls, used to be hidden in the trees. Now Twin Falls is real easy to find.

THE ROAD TO HANA

There are sixteen mile markers from the beginning of the Hana Highway in Ka-hu-lui to the intersection of Kau-pa-kalua Road. It is here that the Hana Highway changes from County Road #360 to County Road #36. After another three mile markers you come to the sign that says: NARROW WINDING ROAD NEXT THIRTY MILES.

It is this sign at the end of the long stretches of paved straightaways extending from Ka-hu-lui through Pa'ia, Ku'au, Ha'i-ku and Huelo that suddenly slows you down from a legal 35 miles an hour to what becomes the long, slow drive to Hana town and the 'Ohe'o Gulch/Ki-pahulu area.

It says "thirty miles" on the sign which some will evaluate as a thirty to forty-five minutes leisurely drive. In reality, or should I say, in Hana Highway time, that adds up to two hours if you do not stop along the way.

Driving an hour and half along the Hana Highway, to Hana town, is a drive that requires vigilance and spontaneity. In addition to the many roadside attractions, which inevitably slow you down, there is also the Road itself. Twisting and winding, (it averages approximately 3 minutes to drive every mile) as you negotiate narrow bridges, hairpin turns, pot holes by the dozen and trucks and cars coming from Hana.

IMPROVING THE ROAD

The Road has been continually improved over the years. As Robert Wenkam in his beautifully photographed and now out of print book, Maui: The Last Hawaiian Place, writes: "When Hana was without a road, and the coastal steamer arrived on a weekly schedule, Hana-bound travelers unwilling to wait for the boat, drove their car to the road's end at Kai-lua, rode horseback to Kau-mahina ridge, then walked

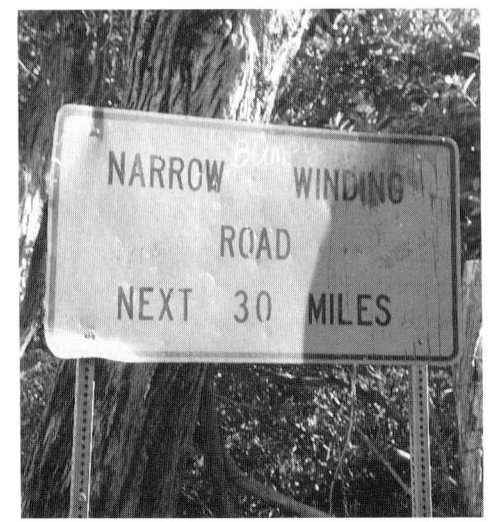

(30) The old sign announcing the beginning of the Road to Hana.

(31) "...waters, white and frothy, rush off the mountain toward the sea....", Wai-kani Bridge, Mile Marker #20.

down the switchback trail into Hono-manu Valley. Friends carried them on flatbed taro trucks across Ke-'anae peninsula to Wai-lua cove. By outrigger canoe it was a short ride beyond Wai-lua to Na-hiku landing where they could borrow a car for the rest of the involved trip to Hana. Sometime the itinerary could be completed in a day. Bad weather could make it last a week."

Even after the road was completed in 1926, "the road was little more than a wide mud and gravel path."

Of course the Road that I first encountered in 1974 had already been greatly improved upon since the 1960's

(32) (33) (34) "...long stretches of paved straight-aways extending from Ka-hu-lui through Pa'ia, Ku'au, Ha'i-ku and Huelo...."

THE NARROW WINDING ROAD * 13

The Road to Hana

(35) Gas tanker on its way to Hana takes up 2/3 of the Road.

before any serious attempt to pave it had begun. At that time, the Road had very few metal guard rails to keep cars from ending in a ditch, no yellow lines to help remind drivers which side to stay on, and only occasional reflectors in particularly difficult sections.

Since the Road was again upgraded in 1982, this formerly twisting and winding, barely graded dirt road has very few sections that remain bumpy and unattended. I sometimes wonder if the bumpy sections that are left, such as the section between Mile Marker #23 to Mile Marker #29, have been left as a reminder of former days.

In the meantime, the Road Crew is constantly filling pot holes, trimming back roadside weeds and clearing fallen rocks and trees. Even by the time the bumpy section is repaved another section is likely to be chewed up and degraded by the constant rains puddling on top or the moisture from the rains seeping beneath the surface undermining its stability.

Nevertheless, with all the refinements of bridge markers, guard rails, numerous reflectors, Yield To On Coming Traffic Signs and other directional indicators designed to minimize accidents on this heavily traversed 'highway,' anyone who drives the Hana Highway for the first, or one thousandth, time will agree with the T-shirt sold at various locations around the island which states: "I Survived The Hana Highway."

THE WAY IT WAS

I remember when it was possible to walk five or six miles without seeing one car. Many times I would stroll along the highway stopping under a mango

(36) Part of the Road has fallen off the cliff.

14 * THE NARROW WINDING ROAD

(37) The Road Crew forever filling pot holes.

tree to search for an unbroken ripe mango among the fallen fruit.

Or, if I happened to have a papaya with me, I might choose a particularly beautiful ocean view, sit on the hillside, cut the papaya open, clean out the seeds and savor each bite as I took in the view. Those were idyllic times for me along the Hana Highway.

CHANGES ARE INEVITABLE

Life in Hana and all of Maui changed radically around 1978 when Time and Newsweek magazines, among others, ran cover stories on the magical island of Maui.

In addition to the numerous cars, the tourist vans have also multiplied from one company called Holo Holo running one or two vans to Hana per day, to several companies running several vans down the Hana Highway each day.

By 1990 it was estimated that 2000 people drive to Hana each week, or 80,000 to 100,000 a year!

This number of people driving out to Hana is likely to increase if those who favor development of Maui into a world class tourist destination have their way.

Recently, the Ka-hu-lui Airport was enlarged and modernized. But the airport runway would still have to be lengthened from 73,000 to 96,000 feet in order to accommodate international flights, specifically giant 747's direct from Japan.

These 747's would bring an additional 500 people to Maui each time a jet landed. Those dependent on tourism, from hotels to vacation rentals, from restaurants to gift shops are clamoring for more customers.

In reality, however, the infrastructure of Maui (roadways, garbage collection, electricity, sewerage and so forth) is already over burdened.

THE BEAUTY OF THE ROAD

Depending on the season, ginger and heliconia (commonly called lobster claw) may be blooming, banyan trees may have berries, shower trees may be resplendent. Edible fruits such as mountain apples may be displaying their fuzzy flowers or dangling their deep, red pear like fruit. Small, red, tart and tasty strawberry guavas may also be ripe for the picking.

(38) Breadfruit, a winter staple in Hawaii and throughout Polynesia.

Then there are the breadfruits which are a native Hawaiian staple. Breadfruit can not be eaten raw but can be cooked into a pudding, sliced and fried like chips, cubed and baked like potatoes and much more. Each fall in Hana, during the Aloha Week celebration, one of the most popular events is the Great Breadfruit Cookoff. Fierce competition. Incredible delicacies. Proud winners.

Of course there are small common mangoes and ordinary yellow guavas all year round though heaviest in August and September. At the right time of year, rose apples are abundant though it is difficult to eat more than one as they taste like roses smell, and eating more than one fruit is like drinking a bottle of rose scented perfume.

Driving the Hana Highway is especially wonderful during a heavy rainfall when the waterfalls become awesome as the waters, white and frothy, rush off the mountain toward the sea.

And on bright sunny blue sky days when you can climb up to the waterfalls that are above the roadside waterfalls to swim in magnificent pools surrounded by wild jungle flowers and foliage.

Driving at night during a Full Moon is especially magical. Full Moon light romantically illuminates the ocean, shines on the foliage and makes strange and sometimes mysterious shadows. On these nights, waterfalls are especially beautiful as you drive toward one and the white water shines brightly in the moonlight.

Sometimes on Full Moon nights the white owl may fly across the Road. Or better still, an owl may fly along the Road in front of you.

The only time the Road is really scary is at night when it rains. When it rains, the Road can be hazardous as rocks fall, land slides, trees topple and visibility seems to be only a few inches ahead. It is at times such as these that those road side reflectors, narrowing road reminders, and black and orange diagonal signs bolted onto each bridge are especially appreciated.

THE ROAD IS THE DESTINATION

As others have pointed out before me, no matter what the weather, no matter what the season, the drive to Hana is always outstanding. It should be understood that even though the Hana Highway takes you from one place to another, the Road itself is the destination.

(39) The beginning of the Road is so well paved that this sign has finally been removed.

(40) Mail boxes at Door of Faith Church Valley in windy Huelo.

(41) Cattle truck parked in the family one car garage. Tight fit. The truck now has a For Sale sign on it.

(42) Truck entering the Hana Highway after unloading aggregate for the Hana-wana Valley driveway.

(43) Base Yard of the East Maui Irrigation Company (EMI), a subsidy of the Alexander & Baldwin Company.

(44) A Hale-a-kala National Park Ranger on his twice annual walk around the circumference of Maui. Good cardio-vascular exercise.

(45) Bamboo forest at Na-ili-ili-ha'ele Bridge, great place to cut bamboo for many uses, Mile Marker #6.

(46) A stand of Rainbow Eucalyptus trees, one of over 55 varieties of eucalyptus growing on the island of Maui.

(47) Handhewn stone walls at Ka-ai-ea Bridge, Mile Marker #16.

(48) Handhewn stone walls are part of the irrigation ditches dug in the 1870's to channel water to the dry side of the island.

(49) "AMARAL" a Portuguese family name carved into a roadside embankment many years ago.

(50) One of many hairpin curves that are without a Hairpin Curve Sign.

DRIVING THE HANA HIGHWAY

Many visitors to Maui driving the Hana Highway understandably meander along enjoying the scenery while absorbing the experience of lush jungle and extraordinary vistas. Every once in a while the relaxed driver will hang out of the car window to catch a glimpse of a strange and exotic tree or shrub. No need to hurry. And every reason in the world not to hurry.

It is understandable that the Hana Highway inspires drivers to be in no hurry. Indeed, it has always bewildered me when tourists don't take their time. I suspect there are some people who never slow down to enjoy the details of life. Perhaps they are just capable of enjoying the wonders of the world with their fast forward button constantly pushed.

Even among slow drivers, it seems there are even slower ones. Senior citizens are especially slow. No longer willing to risk their life for a thrill ride along a narrow winding mountain road, they literally creep along.

Now I've driven the Hana Highway more times than I can count, though I estimate an average of once a week for over twenty years. This adds up to over two thousand trips back and forth.

With all the trips I have made I have come to know the Road intimately. I know the names of bridges, waterfalls and vegetation. Driving the Hana Highway is like driving past old friends knowing that in all likelihood, I will

(51) Wai-ka-moi Bridge, Mile Marker #10

(52) Ko-lea Bridge, almost Mile Marker #13.

20 * THE NARROW WINDING ROAD

see them again and again. Knowing and anticipating road surface, straightaways and hairpin curves, it takes me about an hour and a half to drive from Hana to Pa'ia.

THE RULES OF THE ROAD

When driving the Hana Highway, it is a great treat when I can drive along in a leisurely manner. But this is not always the case. Sometimes I need to zip down the Hana Highway. And, it is at those times that I need to hurry that I appreciate the casual driver who is considerate enough to pull over at one of the many turn outs and let me slide by and go z-o-o-o-m-m-m.

Some folks are not aware of the 'rules of the road' and continue driving slow and steady in a turtle-like way. You would think that someone looking in their rear view mirror seeing another car rapidly approaching would be hint enough that the courteous thing to do is to pull over.

Certainly, it is possible that the slow driving driver did not notice the somewhat rapid approach of another car in their rear view mirror. If this is the case, then certainly driving almost bumper to bumper would be a clear indication that this driver behind them wishes to pass.

Finally, to make the message really clear, intervehicular communication may become necessary. First, there is the flashing of high beams which usually works at night but not always during daylight hours. If this doesn't get the slow driver's attention then a gentle beep on the horn may be needed as a place to pull off the Road is obviously in sight. If this doesn't work after a couple of attempts then it may be necessary to hold the horn button down until the blaring horn shatters the jungle silence and the message to get out of the way becomes really, really clear.

IS IT WORTH THE DRIVE?

One of the popular questions people ask when they are already smack in the middle of Hana town are: "How much further to Hana?" and "Where's Hana?"

Then there is the question of "How much further to the Seven Pools?" The answer to this question can come either in miles or in time. Another fifteen miles afterall doesn't sound too bad. But another half hour to forty minute drive! This news gets eyebrows raised followed by the inevitable next question: "Is it worth the drive?"

Some tourists love the drive along the narrow winding Hana Highway and are dazzled by the vistas, the jungle ambience, the surprises around each wiggle of the Road. Many tourists can not believe they have entered into a picture postcard fantasy of waterfalls, lush jungles, exotic flowering plants, balmy weather and palm trees silhouetted against incredible sunsets. For them the journey was truly "worth" every twist and turn, every bump and every pothole. For them the drive to 'Ohe'o Gulch will be even more thrilling as the Road to 'Ohe'o gets narrower

Driving The Hana Highway

and the scenery greener.

This is not true for everyone. Not everyone enjoys the ride along the Hana Coast Road. Many people have no idea what driving the Hana Highway means in wear and tear. For some people, driving the Hana Highway is an endurance test making them feel battered and brutalized by the time they get back to the comfort of their hotel room or condominium in Ki-hei or La-haina.

In truth, how can anyone say it is "worth the drive" when you look into a car and see one person, face flushed with neck and ears glowing like red light bulbs (apparently with heart problems and high blood pressure), another individual whose face is a bluish-green color (motion sickness?), and yet another, scared of heights and anticipating the worst from a thousand turns and curves, who is now pop-eyed and pale white as a sheet regardless of what color they began the journey as.

To these frazzled travelers you say, "No, the drive is not worth it. It is just more of the same, and the Road gets narrower and even more bumpy. Quite honestly, if you didn't enjoy the Road thus far, you might as well turn around. Afterall, you now have to drive back over the same thirty miles of narrow winding road. And, if you're staying at a hotel in La-haina or Wai-lea, don't forget that's another hour and a half drive. Alo-ha."

It can not be emphasized enough that driving the Hana Highway is an adventure. An adventure anyone can enjoy if they drive slow and steady and stop frequently to enjoy where they are.

(53) Photographing the memories.

(54) A waterfall above a roadside waterfall - Pu-oho-ka-moa Bridge, Mile Marker #11.

(55) This rock was painted white so cars whipping around the corner won't slam into it.

(56) Mighty waterfalls surrounded by lush jungle growth.

(57) 10 a.m. traffic build up at Wai-ka-moi Bridge, almost MM #10.

(58) Pu-oho-ka-moa Stream during heavy rains.

(59) Someone sitting in a jungle shelter watching the waterfall flow.

(60) Each bridge is named and numbered: "360" is the County Road number, "007" is the bridge inventory number.

(61) Pu-oho-ka-moa Bridge built in 1912, Mile Marker #11.

(62) One of these guys is waiting for me to get out of the way so he can take a picture of the waterfall I'm standing on.

(63) Innocence, a sparkling jungle pool surrounded by pristine beauty.

(64) Taking pictures from on top of the falls. Other people dive.

SIGNS OF THE HANA HIGHWAY

WIGGLES - There are 22 signs like this that indicate that the Road continues to continue as a continuously winding Road. This sign informs you that there is no end to the windings in the windings of the narrow winding Road. But how wiggly does a section of Road have to be in order to qualify for the Wiggles Ahead Sign? The section past Wai-ka-moi Ridge Trail turnoff has no wiggles ahead sign as suddenly you either drive slower or fiercely grip the wheel as you determinedly take the curves as a racer in the Maui Grand Prix.

(65) Signs to help you get on the bridge and signs to help you get off.

(66) One of 22 Wiggles Ahead Signs.

ARROWS - These signs come in groups and are apparently designed to guide you around some tight hairpin turns and in general to keep you on the Road at places where there are no soft shoulders. In other words, you're either on the Road or off the Road, and if off, off forever. It is also used in one place coming up from Hono-manu Bridge (which is just before Mile Marker #14). These Arrows are used to keep you from driving into the wall of the mountain.

STRIPES - Diagonal stripes are used as bridge alerts to help you successfully navigate onto the many narrow one lane bridges. These signs are especially helpful at night and even more important during a torrential downpour when these orange stripes are all you can see. If you examine some of the bridges, it becomes quite evident that many a motorist managed to hit the bridge prior to the time these signs were erected (and probably since).

YIELD AHEAD SIGN - I laughed at these signs when they were first put up in the early 1980's. Now as tourist traffic has multiplied, I have come to greatly appreciate these signs as they help the tourist in a hurry to slow

26 * THE NARROW WINDING ROAD

SIGNS OF THE HANA HIGHWAY

(67) Yield Ahead Sign followed by Yield To On-coming Traffic Sign.

down for the inevitable Yield To On-Coming Traffic Sign ahead. This sign is intended to help the driver be aware that the section of the Road coming up will accommodate only one car at a time.

YIELD TO ON-COMING TRAFFIC SIGN - The idea is to yield to on-coming traffic on a section of the Road that is wide enough for only one car. Actually, in some cases, two cars can probably pass safely but might scrape each other. In the old days we used to joke that to drive the Hana Highway it was necessary to grease the driver's side of the car so you could slide by on-coming traffic. Now we have the offspring of modern traffic management, the Yield To On-Coming Traffic Sign. However, as a frequent driver of the Hana Highway, it continues to amaze me how many drivers neglect the opportunity to pause in order to ascertain if indeed there is on-coming traffic to yield to. Instead, those little tourist cars come whipping around the bend into a narrow section of Road, slamming on their brakes when they see another car directly in front of them while their passengers' eyes bulge in fright as they anticipate their demise.

ONE LANE BRIDGE SIGN - Another obvious sign forewarning you to slow down and not hit the bridgework. This sign also is a suggestion to let the car that is already on the bridge get off before you attempt your own crossing. Or, if you are approaching the bridge just a little ahead of a long line of cars coming from the opposite direction, speed up so you can cross it first.

(68) One Lane Bridge Sign.

Signs Of The Hana Highway

NO PASSING ZONE SIGN - These triangular signs are designed to remind you that you are crazy to think you can pass another car without taking your life in your hands as well as jeopardizing the safety of any car that might be coming around the next curve on a narrow stretch of Road. Actually, these signs remind you of the obvious: either drive slow and stay in line or beep the driver in front of you and hope the driver in front of you will pull over and let you go by.

HAIRPIN - There are two of these signs going and two returning from Hana. They are constructed to be larger than other road signs (you might notice that there are two halves to this sign and they are riveted together). These signs are oversized to make sure you pay attention. Of course there are other hairpin turns that are just as radical and do not have a Hairpin Turn Sign to forewarn the driver. There are a few hairpin curves that do not even have Arrows.

FALLING ROCK SIGN - I have driven many highways featuring this sign from Big Sur to the Rocky Mountains but nowhere have I seen as many

(69) (70) (71) Hairpin Turn Signs.

THE NARROW WINDING ROAD

(72) No Passing Zone

piles of rocks along the edge of a road as I have seen along the Hana Highway. I don't mean just a pile of rocks here and there along the side of the Road but I mean significant landslides that have closed the Road for hours as the road crew efficiently and speedily clears the way.

In addition to rocks falling on the Road, the driver has to keep an eye open for branches and whole trees that come crashing down during torrential rains - rains which can last for days.

Frequently mangos and guavas have also landed on the hood of my car but don't expect to see Falling Guava or Falling Mango signs along the Hana Highway. There are also Slow Children and Bad Curve warnings. Which brings up the questions: Why do these children have to go so slow? And why don't they reprimand those curves for being so bad?

ONE WAY SIGNS - These signs prevent accidents each day by helping weary travelers in and out of the park-

(73) Falling Rock Sign.

(74) One Way Signs.

ing lot in front of the comfort station at Pua'a Ka'a State Wayside Park after Mile Marker #22.

THE ROAD NARROWS SIGNS - These signs are self-evident. Notice Photo #1 on the first page of this book of a Road Narrows Sign deep in the rainforest heavily coated with jungle mold.

HA - TO BREATHE OR NOT TO BREATHE

As you drive along the Hana Highway, you might notice open ditches that are marked by signs that say,

PRIVATE PROPERTY
NO SWIMMING
DOMESTIC WATER

It is these ditches and aqueducts, owned and operated by East Maui Irrigation (EMI) that are to some extent the "life blood" of Maui's sugar cane and pineapple industry and now of its hotel and real estate developments.

This elaborate system of ditches and aqueducts which extends along the Hana Coast to the Seven Pools/'Ohe'o Gulch area was conceived in the 1870's by Henry P. Baldwin. It was his idea to bring water from the rainforest to the dry desert side of Maui. In this way the thousands of acres of unused land owned by Henry P. Baldwin's family, under the business firm name, Alexander & Baldwin, Inc., could be made profitable.

When it was completed it was an outstanding engineering accomplishment. The tunnels were dug with pick and shovel and the stone walls that line the canals and serve as retainer walls were all hand hewn. (See Photo #45 & #46)

It was always interesting to me how the name 'East Maui Irrigation' had almost a governmental sound to it, as if it was County or State operated. However, in reality, EMI is a subsidiary of the Alexander and Baldwin Company.

You might say the water bill from EMI is part of the overhead of HC&S (Hawaiian Commercial and Sugar Company), another Alexander and Baldwin subsidiary. As HC&S gets a government subsidy check each year, it uses taxpayers' money to pay EMI. You might say, A & B wins by losing.

The Alexander and the Baldwin families were among the many missionary families who came to the Hawaiian Islands to save the so-called

(75) (76) EMI ditches taking water to the 'other side.' This engineering accomplishment was the brainchild of sugar king, Henry P. Baldwin.

30 * THE NARROW WINDING ROAD

HA - TO BREATHE OR NOT TO BREATHE

heathen population by converting them to the various denominations of Christianity. This was rather easy to do as the traditional Hawaiian social and religious structure was already in major upheaval after the death of King Kamehameha and the coming into power of his queen, Ka'ahumanu (who was born in a cave near Hana Bay). In fact, many Hawaiians thought that the Trinity was just another variation of their own gods Ku, Kane and Lono as these three ancient gods of Hawai'i had similar characteristics and attributes.

The missionaries eventually motivated the Hawaiian people to cover their nakedness, wear shoes, bathe on Saturday instead of swimming and to give up the sacred hula dance along with polygamy, polyandry, gambling and adultery.

The missionaries were also influencial in convincing a segment of the population to give up human sacrifice and poking out their eyes in grief when a loved one died along with a wide variety of nasty black magic games such as 'anana, or praying people to death whom they didn't like.

Not only did the missionaries manage to convince the native Hawaiian people to give up their ancestral religion but they also managed to acquire ownership of native Hawaiian lands. Consequently, the largest land holders on each island are the descendants of the original missionary families.

It was in 1819 that the first missionary doctors arrived. The first to arrive on Maui was the Reverend Spaulding. Soon after his arrival, he became ill and returned to the Mainland to be followed by the Right Reverend Dwight David Baldwin. Reverend D. D. Baldwin stayed and prospered.

The Baldwin family is the most influential family on Maui. Their holdings include: HC&S (Hawaiian Commercial and Sugar Company), EMI (East Maui Irrigation), the Matson Navigation Company, and A&B Properties. It is A&B Properties which were the developers of the Maui Mall in Kahu-lui and of the Wai-lea Beach Resort which is the largest resort on the islands and itself three times the size of Wai-kiki.

(77) Portrait of Rev. D. D. Baldwin, by courtesy of the Lahaina Restoration Society.

Peter Baldwin, the current head of the Baldwin clan, also owns Haleakala Ranch, the fifth largest ranch in the United States which operates the only dairy on Maui. In addition, Peter Baldwin's passion for polo motivated him to develop Maui's world class polo team.

We might also mention the Cameron branch of the Baldwin family headed by Colin C. Cameron and his mother. In 1969, Colin and his mother sold their shares in Alexander and Baldwin to establish another of Maui's most powerful corporations, the Maui Land and Pineapple Company.

It was Henry P. Baldwin, the son of the famous missionary, who first started growing pineapples on his 23,000 acre Hono-lua Ranch and who opened the first cannery in La-haina in 1919. The Maui Land and Pineapple Company recently converted the cannery into a major shopping mall while developing a sizeable chunk of this agricultural land into the ritzy Ka-palua Resort with luxury suites up to $1200 a night.

It was reported in the February 5, 1991 edition of the Maui News in reference to the 1990 earnings of the Maui Land and Pineapple Company that Ka-palua Resort and Ka'ahumanu Shopping Center were again top wage earners while the pineapple division finished another year in the red. This was also the case in 1991, 1992 and 1993.

The Maui News, by the way, is the only daily newspaper on the island and is also owned by the Cameron family, Colin Cameron's sister, Maisey that is.

There was another way the earlier Caucasian visitors rose to status on the islands and that was by marrying an Hawaiian princesses. Charles Reed Bishop was one of these fortunate souls. He eventually became the most prominent banker on the islands. The Bishop Museum and Honolulu's Bishop Street are both named in his honor.

Or, as in the case of Benjamin Dillingham, a stranded sailor who stopped in Honolulu in 1865, to marry the daughter of a missionary. It was the Dillingham Dredging Company that in 1953 was contracted to dig a yacht harbor in Honolulu. Walter Dillingham used the dredgings to fill in a swamp which was later developed as the Ala Moana Shopping Center, one of the largest shopping malls in the world.

Of course it was also helpful to be the son of a missionary as was Sanford Ballard Dole. Sanford Ballard Dole, after participating in the overthrow of the Hawaiian monarchy in the Revolution of Jan 17, 1893, became the first president of the new Republic of Hawai'i, July 4th 1894. Later, when Hawai'i's strategic importance was realized at the outbreak of the Spanish-American War, Hawai'i was annexed as a U.S. Territory, Aug. 12, 1898, and Dole became the first governor of the new territorial government.

As to the matter of Hawai'i Statehood, this was out of the question till the 1950's due to the difficulty the Mainland attitudes had about a state that

HA - To Breathe Or Not To Breathe

had a very mixed population. A population which was largely Asian.

On August 21, 1959, when Hawai'i was accepted as the 50th State of the Union, there were: 32% Japanese, 30% Caucasian, 17% Hawaiian and part Hawaiian, 11% Filipino, 6% Chinese, and 4% other.

Statehood, in the first half of the twentieth century, would also have been difficult for the sugar industry if the more humane and stringent U.S. labor laws were applied with regard to contract labor which was barely better than slavery conditions and which the sugar industry depended upon. These conditions did change by the 1950's as the result of more liberal legislation.

It was another Dole relative, James D. Dole, who developed the pineapple canning company that still bares the Dole family name, though the Dole Company is now owned by the Castle and Cooke Corporation. The Castle and Cooke Corporation also owns many hotels and other prime real estate throughout the islands.

Amos Star Castle was not a missionary but was hired as a mission teacher, who with his wife, became responsible for the education of the young chiefs and chieftesses of the Hawaiian royalty. Samuel Northrup Cooke was a financial agent for the Board of Missions. Both Castle and Cooke came to the island of O'ahu on the same boat.

In 1851, they were both released from the mission and went into the mercantile business establishing the firm of Castle and Cooke. Castle and Cooke is ranked with Alexander and Baldwin among the most powerful corporations on the Hawaiian Islands.

Rev. Baldwin and Rev. Alexander on the island of Maui also went into partnership. In 1862, they received their first assignment which was the translation of the first five books of the Hebrew Scriptures for a new Hawaiian edition of the Bible.

The family's partnership continued when one of Baldwin's daughters married one of Alexander's sons, and when one of Baldwin's sons, married one of Alexander's daughters. Alexander & Baldwin as a company began in 1869.

It is hard to believe the Hawaiians were taken in so easily by these outsiders. In fact, these outsiders were often laughed at and referred to as 'ha-ole.'

Originally, the word ha-ole was used by Hawaiians in reference to all foreigners much the way Roman 'barbarian' and the Jewish 'goyam' were used to designate other nationalities.

In the Hawaiian language 'ha' is the word for breath. Its pictograph is a spiral as it is in many cultures throughout the world. The name Ha-wai'i, if broken into its components is 'ha' meaning breath, 'wai' meaning water and 'i' meaning people. So the name Hawai'i literally means: 'People of the Breathing, or Living, Waters.' And so it is that the Hawaiian people were and are full

HA - To Breathe Or Not To Breathe

of life, playfulness and feeling.

Even the greeting of the Hawaiian people expresses this concept in the word alo-ha. 'Alo' means presence or 'in the face.' Along with 'ha' the word for breath, or Spirit, alo-ha loosely translated means to 'breathe into someone's face' or 'to share Spirit with another.' The word alo-ha is used to mean hello, good-bye, compassion, consideration, best wishes and much more. You can send someone your alo-ha, you can give someone your alo-ha and you can ask someone for their alo-ha.

So in contrast to the loose and flowing 'People of the Breathing Waters,' the buttoned-up-to-their-necks, black frocked and tight waistcoated Caucasian visitors were called ha-ole. Ha-ole, loosely translated, means 'people who do not breathe, or have no breath.'

By the time the English Captain James Cook first landed on the Big Island of Hawai'i in January 1778, there was a population of almost 500,000 na-

(78) Spiral Petroglyph - the symbol of 'ha'

tive Hawaiian people. It is reported that when Captain Cook sailed away, he had left "two ewes, a billy goat, a boar, seeds for pumpkin, melons and onions and venereal disease."

Captain Cook wrote in his journal that he tried to keep his sailors away from the native population but found this impossible to do. The tragic results of this first meeting of the Hawaiian people with the western world were confirmed on his return voyage to what he called the Sandwich Islands (named in honor of his British sponsor, the Earl of Sandwich).

It is also on this second visit that Captain Cook met his fateful demise as a result of a minor disagreement between sailors and natives on the Big Island of Hawai'i. His bones, stripped of all flesh, were eventually returned to his shipmates with great apologies from the local chief of Kila-'uea.

Eventually cholera took its toll and then measles and small pox. By 1804, the population had dropped almost in half to 265,000. By 1835, there were only 135,00 native Hawaiians remaining. By 1909, the census was 30,000 native Hawaiian; 10,000 part Hawaiian. According to the 1980 census, there are only 9,366 individuals remaining who can claim pure Hawaiian ancestry with another 166,087 who were counted claiming part Hawaiian ancestry.

Some pests like scorpions, rats, cockroaches and centipedes were no doubt brought to the islands by accident. But the larvae of mosquito were maliciously dumped into Hawaiian waters by the crewmen of one early sailing ship when a Christian missionary refused to allow native girls to swim out to entertain them.

As Lucia Tarallo Jensen and her Hawaiian artist/activist husband Rocky Jensen state in their book, Men Of Ancient Hawaii: "That which was pilfered more than all else at that time (the "missionary" period) was pride and dignity of the Hawaiian people."

They, as do many who have attempted to revive the pre-missionary Hawaiian heritage, report history differently than the one written by the missionaries and their descendants.

According to the Jensens, "Ka'ahumanu, Ka-mehameha's widow, managed to destroy the beliefs in the very foundation upon which the race was built, by totally tearing down the ethical, religious and cultural structure so needed for a people to survive." She did this first by abandoning the elaborate taboo system and then by converting to Christianity. "This led, in 1893, to the last humiliation, the dethronement of Queen Lili'uokalani and the final rape and plunder of Hawaiian sovereignty in the loss of the Crown lands."

This dethronement was engineered by Sanford B. Dole and members of the ha-ole oligarchy who called themselves "The Committee of Safety," supported by the military presence of the United States of America.

At the time, Queen Lili'uokalani said she surrendered not to the revolutionaries but to the "superior force of the United States of America, whose minister plenipotentiary...has caused United States troops to be landed at Honolulu and declared that he would support the said provisional government...Now to avoid collision of armed forces and perhaps the loss of life...I do yield my authority until such time as the Government of the United States shall, upon the facts being presented to it undo the action of its representatives and reinstate me in the authority which I claim as the Constitutional Sovereign of the Hawaiian Islands."

(79) Queen Lili'uokalani in her western finery.

Queen Lili'u-okalani waited many years, and still the Hawaiian people are waiting.

(80) Kaumahina State Wayside Park offers great scenic vistas and the first restroom since Pa'ia.

(81) Ke-'anae Peninsula in the distance. The Hana Highway can be seen as a line cut into the mountain side.

(82) The narrow winding road winds down the mountain side to sea level before winding up again.

(83) Hono-manu Bay offers camping and winter surfing. One of the last Hawaiian villages was located here.

(84) Many bridges were constructed between 1911 and 1916. Ko-lea Bridge, Mile Marker #13.

(85) This section of Ko-lea Bridge was removed by passing cars and trucks.

(86) Hono-manu Bridge, like most of the bridges to Hana, is barely wide enough for one vehicle to squeeze through, Mile Marker #14.

(87) Looking back across Hono-manu Bay toward Kau-mahina State Wayside Park on the point. The Road cuts an obvious groove.

ORIGINS OF MAUI & THE HAWAIIAN ISLANDS

PLUS A THEORY OF THE ORIGIN OF THE HAWAIIAN PEOPLE

The island of Maui started as a fissure on the ocean floor twenty-five million years ago. It first broke surface about one million years ago.

Maui formed as two separate volcanoes. The oldest, Eke Crater, is more commonly referred to as the West Maui Mountains. Eke is much smaller than the younger Hale-a-kala Crater.

The smaller size of Eke Crater is the result of years of erosion from wind and rain. Hale-a-kala is a little over 10,023 feet high. The top portion of the mountain is often referred to as The Crater but in truth it is actually an "erosional depression."

The lava flow between these craters had joined the two volcanoes to form the island now called Maui. This occurred long before the island was inhabited. It is this isthmus, or so-called valley between the two volcanoes, that has given Maui the name identification, the Valley Isle.

Hale-a-kala means 'House of the Sun.' It is officially considered dormant and is not likely to go off again as the hot magma beneath the ocean floor continues to flow up through the vents on the slopes of Kila-'uea on the Big Island of Ha-wai'i.

The last eruption of Hale-a-kala was in 1790 from a vent on the south end of the island near what is now called Perouse Bay. This is the only eruption in recorded history.

The latest lava flow on the Big Island began in 1984 but in actuality, Kila-'uea has been fairly continuous for over one hundred years.

Each of the Hawaiian Islands began as fissures in the ocean floor eventually rising significantly above the ocean surface.

There is now a new volcano forming. This new volcano is situated 22 miles southeast of the Big Island. This volcano, as reported in the Maui News in December 1990, has already risen approximately 11,200 feet above the sea floor. Its crater summit is still about 3,300 feet beneath the surface of the Pacific Ocean. It will take about 50,000 years before this volcano, named Lo-'ihi, becomes the next Hawaiian Island.

There is an old Hawaiian folktale that Maui, a demi-god in old Hawaiian mythology, is responsible for the islands and atolls that we now call the Hawaiian Islands. The story reports that Maui, while fishing with his brothers, pulled each of the islands to the surface of the ocean with a giant fishhook.

There are many legends involving a mythic god/hero named Maui throughout the south Pacific islands.

The Hawaiian Islands are 2,091 miles southwest of San Francisco, California. There are 132 islands, reefs, atolls and shoals stretching 1,523 miles southeast to northwest which constitute the Hawaiian chain.

Origins Of Maui & The Hawaiian Islands

Only seven islands, the Big Island of Hawai'i, Maui, Lana'i, Moloka'i, O'ahu, Kaua'i, and Ni'ihau are currently being inhabited. Eight, if the United States government ever gives the island of Ka-ho'olawe back to the Hawaiian people.

There was once an attempt to establish a cattle ranch on Ka-ho'olawe around the turn of the century but there was great difficulty trying to do this and so the enterprise was given up.

Ka-ho'olawe, since 1951, has been used by the United States Armed Forces for bombing practice. There are many places on this island that are sacred to the ancient Hawaiian culture and many archeological sites that have been destroyed by the bombing. Finally, after a long drawn out court battle, the bombing has ceased and the island is being returned to the civilian population.

The question still remains unanswered: Who are the Hawaiian people? Where did they originate? And, how did they know there were islands in the middle of the ocean thousands of miles from everywhere else? Did they hear about it from other seafaring nations such as the Marqueseans who visited the islands in A.D. 800 before the ancestors of the modern Hawaiians arrived?

The theory that the Hawaiian people, who are not genetically of Polynesian derivation, may be one of the lost tribes of Israel may not be too far fetched.

Incredibly there are many similarities in language. For example, the magician-priesthood of Israel were called the Kohanim while the magician-priesthood of the Hawaiian people are the Kahuna.

Both Hebraic and Hawaiian people use the word 'mana' to describe Vital Life Force, or Power of Life. Even the Creation Myths and stories of a Great Flood are very similar. Perhaps someday the mystery of the origin of the Hawaiian people will be solved.

In Tales of the Night Rainbow, Pali Jae Lee and Koko Willis of Moloka'i answer the question this way: "They came from everywhere. They are everyone. They are the people whe learned you could live with Alo-ha..."

(88) After days of rain, the water streams off the hillside everywhere bringing mud, rocks and trees with it.

(89) Breadfruit, coconut and beer cans in the back of a pick-up truck under a woven lau-hala mat. Hawaiian staples.

(90) Driving under an archway of trees. Next stop: Ke-'anae Arboretum at the next turn of the Road.

(91) Great hiking trails into an Hawaiian rainforest featuring many labeled plantings of native Hawaiian flora, after Mile Marker #15.

(92) One of many unusual looking varieties of flowering wild roadside ginger.

(93) The sweetest smelling ginger is yellow ginger which grows in abundance along the Hana Highway.

(94) At the Ke-'anae Peninsula Exit. 18 miles remaining in the drive to Hana. Average: 3 minutes per mile.

(95) Local residents working in a taro patch on Ke-'anae Peninsula just as many generations before them had worked this land.

(96) *The leaves of the taro plant are steamed while the root is pounded into a paste called poi. Three day old poi is best. "Mo' sour, mo' power."*

(97) *Local gathering of residents for a lu'au under the coconut trees at the water's edge.*

(98) *Ke-'anae Congregational Church was built in 1860.*

(99) *Horse tethered in a jungle clearing. Many local residents use their horses to ride up the slopes of Hale-a-kala in the hunt for wild pig.*

(100) Mud puddles on a dirt road connecting taro fields in Ke-'anae.

(101) One of many romantic and idyllic spots to park your rent-a-jeep. A hala tree and a young coconut tree growing on the edge.

(102) The Ke-'anae Peninsula as seen from the scenic outlook further along the Hana Highway.

(103) Upper Ke-'anae with Hale-a-kala 10,023 foot rim again dominating the distant landscape.

Half Way To Hana

Along the Hana Highway in the town of Ke-'anae is the Wai-anu Fruit Stand that boasts: Half Way To Hana. There's room for vans and cars to pull over, a cold soda vending machine, pay telephone, picnic table, shaved ice, chips and some fresh homemade banana bread. However, for someone who travels the Hana Highway frequently, the question arises: half way from where is the Half Way to Hana refreshment stand? And half way to where? It's more than half way to Hana town and not even close to half way to my house.

UNCLE HARRY'S

Still in Ke-'anae and a little further up the Road, is Uncles Harry's refreshment stand. Uncle Harry passed away recently and this roadside stand is his memorial. Harry Mitchell was greatly loved as an elder who helped to preserve the Hawaiian hertiage. At one time he was asked to teach at the University of Hawai'i. He was one of the few ku-puna (elders) who knew how to navigate by the stars. I called him once to ask about a certain tradition. He explained for a half an hour how he could not answer my question because I didn't speak the 'language.' Nevertheless, I wish I had my tape recorder turned on as the things he said had such deep and profound significance. He and his son, Kimo, who mysteriously disappeared several years ago (some suspect he was murdered), were very active in getting the United States government to give the island of Ka-ho'olawe back to the Hawaiian people.

(104) Wai-anu Fruit Stand, time to stop for refreshments.

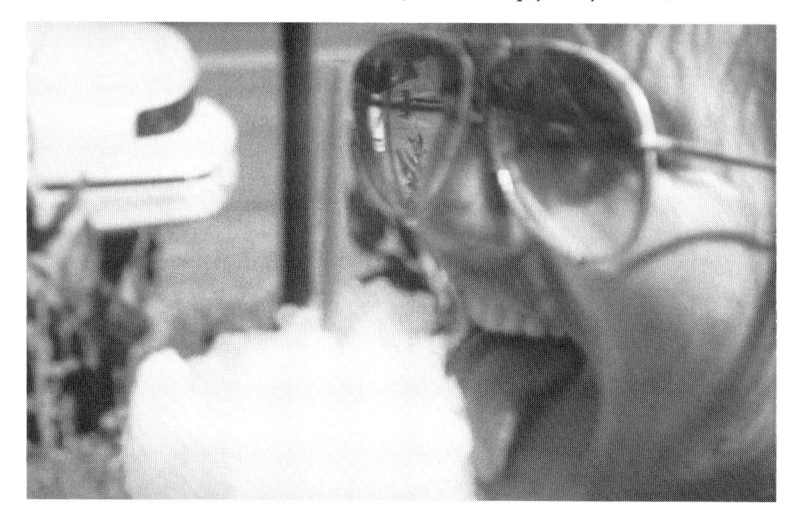

(105) Licking Shaved Ice - Half Way to Hana.

(106) Roadside palm frond weaver just after the Wai-anu Fruit Stand and just before Ke-'anae Elementary School.

(108) Woven palm frond products are versatile and long lasting. An ancient craft that has few modern day practitioners.

(107) The hand greeting in this picture is commonly used as a greeting and to convey the message 'hang loose.' In olden times, the Hawaiian Ka-huna (shaman / magician / priest) held two long leaves of the Ti plant by their stems so they would stick out in opposite directions like the pinky and the thumb depicted here. On the appropriate occasions, the Ka-huna would chant a blessing for peace and well-being and then shake the Ti leaves and clear all negative energy.

The Ka-huna taught that emotions also have substance. Though unlike physical substances, emotional substance is invisible to the two eyes. Ti leaves were used because of their ability to attract emotional substance. Many American Indians use an eagle feather in much the same manner. The Hawaiian word for this sticky emotional stuff is 'aka.' It is also for this reason that many Hawaiian dwellings have rows of green Ti plants growing along certain sides of the house in order to balance the flow of energy.

Ti leaves were also used to make sandles as they were very durable and resisted wear and tear even when walking on highly abrasive lava rocks. Ti leaves were used to make hula skirts.
Even today the leaves of the Ti plant are used to wrap items of food which will be cooked in earthen ovens as Ti leaves will not burn.

(109) This sign is often seen but rarely stopped at. Wai-lua Overlook offers one of the most spectacular views up and down the coast.

(110) Stairway to hilltop observation point cut through tangly, unpenetrable hau branches. Hau is the ancestor of the hibiscus.

(111) Beyond this gate is the road that leads into Wai-lua Valley.

(112) Wai-lua Valley is remote and magical even on a stormy day. It seems like the mystical, hidden valley of Shangri-La.

Aloha Donny, the Tour Guide, says: In 1860, the Catholics of this Valley wanted to build a church, so they petitioned the local Archdiocese but there was no money, so they did the next best thing they could, they had a pray-in. They prayed for three days and three nights & when they went to sleep on the third night, an incredible storm blew up along with a tremendous amount of thunder & lightning. Now we're in the middle of the Pacific, 2400 miles from San Francisco so weather here is quite different than what you have on the Mainland. We don't get alot of thunder & lightning. When we do get thunder it is loud and exciting just like on the Mainland. But lightning, is rare. But when we do get a lightning storm, the whole horizon lights up & you can see the lightning bolts crackle in the sky & come down. Well this storm lasted all night and the waves crashed against the shore. By morning when the storm cleared, they all went down to the shoreline & they saw that an abundance of coral had been washed ashore. Now, we're only a half a million years old on this side of the island and not old enough to have a large coral reef off shore. Yet a large amount of coral had washed ashore. So they took this as a sign from God & gathered all the coral they could. When they went back the next day to gather more coral, there was none left. The coral had been washed back to sea. So they pulverized the coral they had into a fine powder & had just enough to use as stucco paste for the white church you see down there, Saint Gabriel's, The Coral Miracle Church.

(113) Aloha Donny, the Tour Guide, giving his rap to his tour van passengers on the miracle that occurred one night on Wai-lua Peninsula.

(114) Looking up to Wai-lua Overlook from Wai-lua Peninsula standing in front of Saint Gabriel's, The Coral Miracle Church.

(115) The Lady Fatima Shrine, 1862, located next to St. Gabriel's Church on Wai-lua Peninsula.

ISLAND POLITICS

"UA MAU KE EA O KA AINA I KA PONO" - *"the Life of the Land is perpetuated in righteousness"*
--- *Hawaiian State Motto*

Much of island politics happens behind closed doors. Island politicians/power brokers, like their Mainland counterparts and no doubt politicians in countries around the world, know the way to get their policies and bills endorsed is to do it without inviting the public in on the process.

When the public gets involved, compromise is usually necessary. In this way all the special interest groups are included. This of course is the backbone of the democratic process - representation, compromise and majority rule.

On the islands, as elsewhere, the democratic process is often ignored. As elsewhere, the principle, "Profit for the few, at the expense of the many" seems to determine what gets done and how soon.

For instance, there is the example of the Minit Stop fast food store which was given a permit to operate on that section of the Hana Highway which is the main street of the old sugar cane town of Pa'ia. When the shopkeepers and residents of Pa'ia got wind of this agreement they went to court. They were outraged by the idea of a glowing plastic facade joining the weathered and wind beaten wood facades that have bordered the main street of Pa'ia for decades. They wanted to preserve Pa'ia's historical appearance and authenticity.

The community of Pa'ia managed to stall construction for a short time before the inevitable was to happen. It should be noted that the Minit Stop does not have a neon and plastic facade and has done much to replicate the historical look/feel of the original structures. With a little wind, rain and baking hot sunshine, the Minit Stop facade will look like it always belonged. Except of course for those glaring bright lights inside.

Then there is Kihei. As a result of "the grab for profit," we have the current condition of Kihei.

George Cooper and Gaven Daws, the authors of the book, Land And Power In Hawaii, further state: "Like Ka'anapali, Kihei had a master plan. Unlike Ka'anapali, the Kihei master plan did not work....On the contrary, Kihei promptly became the outer islands' outstanding example of continuous, high density lateral coastal sprawl, with a barrier of close set moderately high rise condominiums and hotels blocking off the ocean view."

They then quote travel reporter for the Chicago Tribune, Jerry Hulce, who wrote way back in 1975: "Not even their romantic names can disguise the disregard for the surrounding landscape. They seem to be joined together in a contest of bad taste...." Unfortunately the situation continues to worsen.

Cooper and Daws then document how almost everyone who owned land in Kihei either was in government including then Mayor Elmer Cravalho and Chief of Police Abe Aiona, or had a close relative in government responsible for issuing permits or approving zoning. Needless to say, other rural sections of Maui fear the same onslaught of uncontrolled development.

ISLAND POLITICS

And the list can go on and on. Although store permits and land finagling is seemingly most pertinent to an individual island, some schemes can be devastating not only to all the islands but to the whole world.

GEOTHERMAL

We come now to the controversy involved in the attempt to establish a geothermal site on the Big Island of Hawai'i.

Just as small corporations make big money from fast food and minute stop franchises located in every neighborhood, so the huge corporations make even bigger money installing massive operations involving public utilities.

As fossil fuels are rapidly being depleted and their negative effects on the environment are being realized, the search is on for new methods to generate power. Power to run our electronic toys, appliances and equipment at home and in the business world.

The concept of geothermal is one of many attempts to solve the energy consumption problem of modern technology. Simply put, the idea is to dig wells deep into the earth's volcanic crust so that the steam coming up these holes will turn generators with the generated electricity then being cabled to the various islands.

Unfortunately, the development of a 500 watt geothermal site in the Hawaiian Islands represents the destruction of 5,000 acres of the Wao Kele O Puna rainforest on the Big Island of Hawai'i.

The Puna rainforest, in addition to its ecological role in breathing oxygen into our fragile atmosphere, is also sacred to the Hawaiian people. It has been for many hundreds of years a place to worship, to gather ceremonial and medicinal herbs as well as the natural habitat of several species of native flora and fauna which will be threatened with extinction.

Not only that, but there is no guarantee that such a project will be sustainable for many years to come which will mean digging new geothermal holes which means more labor, more money and continued profits for big corporations. And continued loss of valuable rainforest.

The irony is of course that the United States, as "an environmentally conscious nation," is urging other countries, such as Brazil, not to destroy their precious rainforests!

Not only does the presence of over 200 steam wells and generating plants endanger the natural habitat of rare Hawaiian species, but the electromagnetic fields generated by the high voltage transmission lines are a risk to residents of the area as well.

In addition, the electromagnetic radiation from the 480 miles of undersea cables may effect the Humpback whales ability to navigate in an area known to be prime breeding grounds as well as destroy the valuable fishing grounds of Maui's Ahihi Bay and Molokai's Penguin Banks.

In the January 1991 issue, the Hawaii Eco Report pointed out: "The closed door nature of the State's efforts to promote this project is painfully obvious in the documents obtained in the discovery phase of this litigation. Massive amounts of taxpayer's money is being used to sell us a product before it is known whether geothermal is either economical or desirable to develop. To use the taxpayer money to launch premature public relation campaigns for a project designed to benefit private parties is a clear sign that the public's interest are taking a back seat to private development."

In other words, until environmentally conscious organizations such as the Greenpeace Foundation-Hawaii, the Blue Ocean Preservation Society and the Sierra Club brought this controversy to the public's attention, no environmental impact study had been made in accordance with the National Environmental Policy Act. Once again, politics behind closed doors.

While all this controversy rages, the experimental wells that have already been dug have exploded twice in 1991.

As of this writing, the last explosion was on the New Moon night of June 12, 1991, resulting in a massive evacuation of the surrounding area as massive quantities of hydrogen sulfide gases spewed over the countryside.

None of this was reported in any of the local newspapers. I found out from a friend who resides just ten miles down the road.

SUGAR

Sugar cane burning is the largest cause of pollution on the islands and contributing factor in many health problems reported by island residents. For years a small minority of Maui residents have lobbied to terminate this environmentally insane and unhealthy practice of sugar cane burning.

The irony about sugar cane burning is that the D.O.H. (Department of Health) had ordered the sugar cane companies to cease sugar cane burning in 1971! This news was reported in the Honolulu-Star Bulletin, February 9, 1971. Yet nothing has been done to enforce this Department of Health decision.

The reason sugar cane fields are torched is ostensibly to burn off the leaves before the sugar cane is hauled off to the mills for processing. The logic is obviously to remove and dispose of the green matter before hauling. In

(116) Wire mesh aluminum can catchers are seen around the island encouraging recycling.

(117) Pu'u-nene Mill processes sugar cane twenty-four hours a day. Canal (left foreground) takes foul smelling fertilizer to the cane fields.

(118) Cane fields are set a flame to remove the green matter before hauling the cane to the mill. PVC pipes and pesticides go up in smoke.

(119) Spraying sugar cane fields with CP3.

(120) Acres of sugar cane. At one time Sugar was King. Now it is a government subsidy crop having difficulty competing in the world market.

ISLAND POLITICS

other words, trash the trash and haul only the moneymaking sugar cane.

However, besides the green matter releasing ash into the atmosphere, the pesticides which have been sprayed on the plants are also released into the air. If that is not bad enough, the PVC pipes used to irrigate the fields also go up in flames releasing their deadly carcinogenic toxins into the air to settle in the lungs of those living in surrounding residential areas. Among other toxins, sugar cane burning releases silicon dioxin which has been linked to the high incidence of people with respiratory diseases on the island.

The reality is that those in control of the sugar companies receive a substantial government subsidy. Apparently, both the sugar and pineapple industries have trouble competing with third world countries which sell sugar and pineapple in the world marketplace for considerably less. So though we pay less for sugar and pineapple in the store, we pay more for it in taxes.

Once again we have a situation of ensconced bureaucracy lobbing to keep its wheels turning simply because those wheels are already turning.

PINEAPPLE

After the first fruit is picked, each pineapple plant will produce two smaller size fruits. As these smaller fruits are not as commercially valuable as the first larger one, the pineapple companies usually cut off the fruit and then plow the rest of the plant back into the soil along with the sheets of black plastic used when the pineapple tops were first stuck in the ground.

Commercially grown pineapple, like many commercially grown fruits, are picked green to ensure longer shelf life after they are shipped to the markets. When picked green, fruits never achieve their full ripeness. This means the fruit acids of the prematurely picked fruit never quite convert to sweet tasting fruit sugars.

Every once in a while I am told about, or am fortunate enough to discover, an unsprayed pineapple field. It seems the local pineapple company allow certain fields from time to time to lie fallow after they harvest the first fruiting.

When a field is going to be left to a natural cycle, and not harvested for commercial use, pesticide sprays are not used. When unsprayed, even the smaller second and third fruiting are sweeter, tastier and juicier than those pineapples sprayed and picked green.

Indeed, it is quite possible, and very enjoyable, to eat a whole pineapple without having gums and lips blister as usually happens when eating two or three slices of a highly acidic, pesticide sprayed pineapple which was picked prematurely.

At one time the island of Lana'i was known as the Pineapple Island as the entire island was used solely for the production of pineapple. James D. Dole (another descendant of the Dole missionary family) purchased the island in 1922 for one million dollars. The Dole Company's Lana'i holdings were eventually consumed by the Castle & Cooke Company whose holdings were eventu-

ISLAND POLITICS

(121) Pineapple

ally consumed by California billionaire, David Murdoch.

Apparently, David Murdoch closed the pineapple plantation because it was cheaper to grow pineapples elsewhere. No mention was ever made of the health hazards of cancer and fetal malformation which were being related to the intense use of agricultural pesticides.

Now, one side of Lana'i is being developed as a playground for the rich and famous with two very fancy and expensive hotels. While eight acres on the northeast shore across the Auau Channel opposite Maui has been developed as the Club Lana'i.

PINEAPPLE AND SUGAR

Pineapple and sugar cane cultivation on the Hawaiian Islands will soon be history. It has become financially impossible for either of these agricultural industries to compete with the lower prices offered for these crops by many third world countries. The only thing that keeps either of these crops still operative is government subsidies - money supplied by taxpayers.

Not only are the pineapple and sugar industries of Hawai'i the largest sources of air and earth pollution, but both sugar and pineapple use valuable agricultural land that could be used to farm fruits, vegetables or industrial hemp for local consumption. Hemp can be used for paper, resins, biomass and has thousands of other commercial uses.

It is astounding that on Maui produce sold in the chain supermarkets are imported from the Mainland! Amazing that the chain supermarkets offer bananas from Costa Rica, avocados from Mexico, lettuce and other greens from various agricultural centers throughout mainland United States. Only the smaller family owned local markets offer produce which is grown on Maui, and usually at more reasonable prices.

For years a small segment of the population realizing the need to convert sugar and pineapple land into usable farm land have screamed into deaf ears. The voice of the people in recent years has grown stronger and it is now just a matter of time before the sugar and pineapple bureaucrats give up their dependency on the U.S. government to subsidize their income. This is just another case where government pays big business to maintain the façade that they are big business when actually they are just big welfare state recipients who receive bigger welfare checks.

THE NARROW WINDING ROAD * 53

(122) The Road winds up from Wai-lua Peninsula through dense rainforest.

(123) Flatbed laden with groceries destined for the Hana store. Everything that gets to Hana gets there by traveling the Hana Highway.

(124) Who can say for sure what this truck does and why it's going to where it's going.

(125) Many ways to travel the Hana Highway. These Canadians are probably biking their way around the world.

(126) Pua'a Ka'a, Rolling Pig State Wayside Park and public restroom.

(127) Wai-o-hu-e Bridge at Pua'a Ka'a State Wayside Park, Mile Marker #22.

(128) Mile Marker #23 to Mile Marker #29 is non-stop bumpy. On this day the potholes were filled with rain water.

(129) Road crew on the way to clear a mud slide further down the Road.

BAMBOO

There are two varieties of bamboo that grow abundantly on Maui: green *Bambusa vulgaris* and green stripe, *Bambusa aureo-variegata*. At the Ke-'anae Arboretum you can also see big black bamboo from the Big Island. There are over a 1,000 varieties and all are relatives of sugarcane and corn. But only green stripe and common green bamboo grow wild on Maui.

Green stripe is often used as a hedge or in a contained placement as it grows in tight clumps. This variety is called monopodal which means 'one footed'.

Green bamboo is the most common variety found on Maui. It is polypodal, or 'many footed' and spreads quickly in all directions and can cover acres.

The extensiveness of a polypodal bamboo forest is obvious after you drive past the EMI base yard at Kai-lua, past the Kai-lua Bridge and down toward the Na-ili-ili-ha'ele Bridge after Mile Marker #6. It is also quite visible if you stop to enjoy the overlook on the Wai-ka-mo'i Ridge Trail after Mile Marker #9 and before the Wai-ka-mo'i Bridge.

It is also evident if you hike up to Wai-moku Falls in the Hale-a-kala National Park area of 'Ohe'o Stream. These are some of the largest bamboo forests on the island that are easily accessible from the Hana Highway.

The bamboo forest after Kai-lua at the Na-ili-ili-ha'ele Bridge is a popular place for residents from all over Maui to harvest bamboo poles to be used as building materials such as fence building or holding up canopies for lu'aus as well as fishing poles.

Many local people harvest bamboo poles by using a cane knife filed to razor blade sharpness. The cane knife is swung high over the head. As it comes down, it is not necessary to come down hard, but more important to hit the bamboo at the correct angle.

By slashing downward at the proper angle, the cane knife cuts cleanly through the entire diameter of the bamboo pole in one stroke. At the wrong angle, the blade will bounce right off.

(130) Green stripe bamboo is mono-podal.

Once the cut is made a point remains sticking upward which can be deadly if anyone was unfortunate enough to stumble and fall.

I always use a bow saw making a cut right below one of the knocks closest to the ground. Beside being close to the ground, using a bow saw leaves a flat surface.

A few years ago, I built a 12' by 12' bamboo platform. This platform required over fifty poles each approximately two to three inches in diameter. I lashed these poles down with #21 nylon twine to sixteen larger poles five inches in diameter laid crosswise. These larger support poles were first lashed to five straight debarked eucalyptus poles each approximately a foot in diameter. Lashing the bamboo poles together in this manner makes a very tight, immovable grid.

If the bamboo is protected from changes in the weather and properly cured, a platform made in this way can last twenty or more years. The eucalyptus poles will also last for many years if soaked in kerosene or paint thinner to discourage boring bugs.

Harvesting this many poles and hauling them home to Hana required two trips. I harvested half the amount one day and returned the next day to harvest the rest.

When I went back to cut the additional twenty-five or so poles, a young Hawaiian guy came over to me. He was holding his cane knife in hand as he too was harvesting bamboo that day. He began thanking me for using the bow saw and making my cuts flat instead of local style, on an angle.

Apparently, just before I arrived he stumbled while working and fell. He said for a moment he thought for sure his life was ending. He was very appreciative that of all the bamboo spears in that location pointing upward, he fell on a bamboo stump that I had cut.

(131) Common green bamboo is poly-podal.

In contrast to common green bamboo, green striped bamboo has a thicker wall which makes it even stronger for use in construction. However, unlike the common green variety which has leaves and branches growing like a pompom only at the narrowest end near the very top, green stripe bamboo has gnarly branches at every knock from top to bottom making it very tedious and scratchy to prepare.

In Japan, as in other Asian countries, bamboo has for centuries been used to construct just about everything. It has been used in the construction of homes, bridges, furniture, water wheels, chimes, decorative items, chop sticks, etc. I have even seen pictures from Japan of skyscraper scaffolding many, many stories high constructed solely of bamboo poles tied together.

As I mentioned, if bamboo is properly protected from the weather, especially weather alternating between wet and hot, bamboo will not splinter or crack and it will maintain its structural integrity for twenty or more years.

After cutting, bamboo is prepared by first allowing it to dry for two weeks. This is best done by standing it upright in a shady location. During this time the green color fades and a shade of yellow/tan appears. By standing the bamboo upright, all the moisture drains downward.

When the bamboo is sufficiently dried, each pole is then passed through the flames of a fire. By passing the bamboo repeatedly through the flames of a fire, the natural oils within the bamboo are brought to the surface appearing like beads of sweat. These oils are then rubbed back into the outer surface with a soft cotton cloth providing the bamboo poles with a protective coating and glistening sheen.

Bamboo has one other major use in the regions of the world where it grows, and to those areas of the world to where it is imported. Bamboo is also used as food. Bamboo shoots appear abundantly in the spring time and are gathered as an addition to many nourishing dishes.

Last May, my eleven year old son went on a field trip with his fifth grade-class to the 'Ohe'o Stream area of Hale-a-kala National Park and was shown by his guide how to gather bamboo shoots. He was shown how to snap the young shoot, twist the sheath to reveal the tasty core. Then, he was told that before eating it was necessary to soak the bamboo shoot in clear water for several hours to leach out the astringent alkaloids which otherwise make the young bamboo shoots taste bitter. After they have soaked sufficiently, the bamboo shoots are simmered and seasoned to taste.

THE COCONUT PALM TREE

What would a picture postcard fantasy of Hawaii be without a palm tree silhouetted against a dazzling sunrise or sunset?

The palm at one time was integral to everyday survival on the Hawaiian Islands and all the islands stretching across Polynesia and Southeast Asia.

Of the hundred's, or is it thousand's, of varieties, only one grouping, *Cocos nuciferas*, grows the edible coconut. Almost all palms have leaves which can be used for roofing, woven mats, removable wall panels or some form of decoration. Only the coconut tree is traditionally planted with the birth of each child.

It is said that the coconut palm has the same life span as the human. By planting a tree when the child is born assures that the new born will have all that is necessary for survival: leaves for the roof and walls and mats for the floors, nut meat & milk for nourishment, coconut shell for bowls and digging tools, and the husk which could be made into twine.

Twine is made by rubbing the oily strands of coconut fiber together between the palm of the hands. The strands are rolled back and forth until they intertwine. Adding additional strands of coconut fibers determines desired thickness or can be added to extend the length. The Coconut Palm was essential to island life.

(132) Cocos nuciferas provides everything you need for a lifetime provided you choose to live a simple life.

Lower Na-hiku Road

Quite honestly, don't bother driving down this road. It really doesn't go any where. Except down, down, down, down. To explore this road requires more time than anyone should bother using up.

In the early 1900's, there was an attempt to establish a rubber plantation down here. The rubber plantation attracted a fairly large population of workers. But the plantation was unsuccessful and couldn't compete with rubber plantations in other countries. When the plantation closed almost all of the people left, leaving a pleasant mix of local and ha-ole. Unless you know someone who lives down this road, there is no place to go and nothing special to see.

True at the very bottom of this three mile long narrow winding road is a fabulous artesian well and swimming hole. But so what? Why drive half an hour to forty-five minutes to jump in for a swim? There is no place to camp out so you can only get wet, get dry and drive back up the long winding road that you just drove down. And, I assure you, it takes longer to drive up the road then it does to roll down, down, down it.

The only other reason you may have for driving down this road is to look at another of the oldest churches on the island.

So take my advice, don't drive down the Lower Na-hiku Road. If you're smart, you'll just look at these pictures and drive past the Lower Na-hiku Exit (unmarked) and continue on to Hana.

(133) Lower Na-hiku Exit to the left; Hana to the right.

60 * THE NARROW WINDING ROAD

(134) Lower Na-hiku Church.

(135) Artesian well at the end of the Lower Na-hiku Road.

(136) Banyan tree across from the old church.

(137) Taking in the coastal view from the bottom of the Lower Na-hiku Road.

(138) Waterfall at Ka-pa'ula Bridge, Mile Marker #23.

(139) Ancient Ohi'a tree overhanging Ka-pa'ula Bridge.

(140) Pu-pa-pe Bridge just before Alii Gardens, Mile Marker #27. Out of the shadows of the jungle and into the light of day once again.

(141) One of the many commercial producers of exotic flowers open to the public.

(142) Robusta eucalyptus trees were planted to provide fuel to heat the pots that the sugar was boiled in at the early sugar mills.

(143) Mufflers, tailpipes and other car parts are often seen rusting along the Road to Hana. Especially between Mile Marker #23 to #29.

(144) Lans Coconut Candy 4 Sale. Lan also sells fresh fruits, flowers and chilled coconuts.

(145) Moku-le'hua Bridge, Mile Marker #28.

(146) A roadside stand selling ginger flowers -
PUT MONEY IN BOX, $1.00 A BUNCH.

(147) Upper Na-hiku is just around the next curve.

(148) Coming out of the Na-hiku Rainforest, Hana is just over the distant hill. Only another 15 minutes of slow driving.

(149) Hana Airport is perched on a lava rock cliff way down below. Only small aircraft are permitted to land here.

(150) Rastabro John's car parked along the Road. He's got alot to say.

(151) Old corral in Hana pasture across from the Hauoli Lio (Happy Horse) Renting Stable and Riding Rink.

(152) Cast iron bathtubs like this one can be seen in many pastures as a rain water catch drinking trough for grazing cattle or horses.

(153) Passing the Hana Airport Road, Hana only three more miles to go.

WAI-'ANAPANAPA STATE PARK

Wai-'anapanapa State Park provides excellent picnic and camping facilities in a well kept park setting. The horseshoe shaped beach is black sand which is finely ground volcanic cinder.

One of the nature trails takes you along the coast all the way to Hana. Another nature trail loops through the park and passes the Queen's Pool. Legend has it that the pool turns red each year in memory of the Queen who was killed in it by her jealous husband. The red color is actually due to a certain species of shimp which spawns in the pool during a certain time of the year.

Contact the State Department of Parks in Wai-lu-ku for permits to use the camp ground or cabins. You can get the cabins for three days maximum. It used to be unlimited until a group of people took advantage of the low rent. The system was changed when a lady in the group had a baby in one of the cabins.

(154) Picnic grounds are constantly manicured.

(155) Excellent place to pitch a tent, except when it rains; and when it rains, it can rain and rain and rain.

(156) This photo does not do Wai-'anapanapa justice. It's beautiful black sand horseshoe shaped beach is exquisite.

(157) Hana High and Elementary school buses, ready and waiting.

(158) Entering the Hana High and Elementary School grounds. The dragon is the school mascot.

(159) The Hana School Gymnasium, the tallest building in Hana.

(160) The Community/School Library is a great facility for cultural concerts, video viewing, research, dark room, etc. etc.

Life In Hana

(161) Hana Ranch lands are some of the richest in the world. The cross made of lava blocks you see on the top of this hill opposite the main entrance of the Hotel Hana-Maui is in memory of Paul Fagan, the man who converted the failing sugar plantation into the very successful Hana Ranch, Hotel and Land Company.

Often tourists who arrive into Hana town inquire: "Do you live here?" When you answer, "Yes," they then inevitably ask, "What do you do for entertainment?"

True indeed, there is no "entertainment" in Hana, if by entertainment you mean theaters, restaurants, dance halls and amusement parks. In fact, the Hana Movie Theater closed in 1974 after a run of Kung-fu and other C-grade films like Beneath Atlantis.

The last movie poster advertised "THE WIZ IS COMING! THE WIZ IS COMING!" But The Wiz never made it. Before The Wiz (a musical remake of the Wizard of Oz with Diana Ross and Michael Jackson) ever made it to Hana, the projector broke and while it was being repaired, Cable T.V. arrived. VCR's were also becoming increasingly popular. Soon there really was no need for a movie theater in Hana.

For many years since it closed, the old movie theater has been used for storage by the Hana Ranch/Hana Hotel/Hana Land Company which owns just about all the available commercial zoned property in Hana except for Hasegawa's General Store and the one Chevron gas station.

For many people entertainment in Hana is provided by the love of beautiful beaches and pools, for some fishing, and for others, jungle hiking. However, the real entertainment in Hana is the people. Not that they are so unusual or bizarre but rather because they are warm hearted and creative.

The best restaurants in Hana are in the homes of the people who live in Hana. Lacking other distractions, Hana residents have cultivated the art of gourmet cooking. Whether a special event like a baby's first year lu'au or a simple gathering of friends, food in a variety of preparations is always in great abundance. Every meal seems like a feast. Potlucks are very popular on Maui and an easy way to have the opportunity to sample many favorite reci-

(162) Two eateries in Hana: the high class pricey Hotel restaurant and the ever popular Hana Ranch buffet. There is also Tutu's Take-out at Hana Bay and sandwiches at Hasegawa's and the Hana Store.

pes from soups and entrees to desserts.

However, I remember one Christmas Day potluck gathering when by coincidence everyone brought their favorite dessert. No soups, salads, entrees. Only fabulous, delicious desserts. Reminds me of the bumper sticker: "Life is Uncertain, Eat Dessert First."

It should be mentioned that the Hana Ranch Restaurant does offer Pizza Night on Thursdays. On Fridays and Saturdays they often feature a buffet dinner along with live music which can range from traditional Hawaiian slack key, country western to reggae or just plain old rock 'n' roll.

There is also entertainment at the Hotel Hana-Maui on Sunday nights. Every other Sunday there is Ke-iki Hula (ke-iki means children), featuring the young children members of the local Hula Ha-lau (ha-lau means school). The little kids, blond haired ha-ole angels and dark haired native Hawaiian angels, wear grass skirts and tell stories with their hands and bodies. As they dance, their teacher, or one of the older children, taps out the beat on a hollowed out gourd while chanting the words to an ancient song.

Apart from the occasional music nights at the Hana Ranch Restaurant, there are no concert halls to go to. So once again the best musical offerings are found among friends. Many residents of Hana are fine musicians who could easily have made the grade as professionals, and some who have.

Even though Hana can boast of some superb guitarists, flute players and 'ukulele pluckers, there are always visitors passing through as a guest of someone who lives in Hana to provide a change of pace.

But most of the local people do for entertainment what millions of other typical American families do. They watch Cable T.V. (only one regular station can be picked up in Hana) or rent a video from Hana Store or from Hasegawa's General Store then sit back, drink beer, eat chips, salted peanuts and pretzels and 'talk story' during the commercial breaks.

'Talk story' is pidgin for people getting together relaxing, hanging out and rambling over a wide range of subjects

Life In Hana

from politics to local gossip, latest family drama to what happen during the day's work. 'Talk story' is a way of revealing oneself. A way to drop barriers of isolation. A way to express feelings. It's a way of getting to know a person by hearing how they sound, listening to the way they think, understanding what's important to them.

And of course there's baseball. Team jerseys are worn as the Hana teams square off against each other at the Hana Ball Park situated next to the tennis courts behind the Hotel Hana-Maui.

Some fierce games have been played. To listen to the guys talk about a game, sounds like war stories.

One tournament is called Mountain Ball which refers to the style of pitching underhand. As I haven't followed baseball since teenager years, Mountain Ball at first seemed really strange. The best I can fathom is that the Mountain Ball style of pitching makes it easy for the batters to hit the ball and run around the bases, this in turn guarantees lots of running, catching, and throwing of the ball around the field. The 1991 teams are: DaBoyz, Eleus, 69ers, the Hawaiians, the Rangers, the Kamanas and the Na-hiku Dinosaurs.

There is also Hana basketball. The teams this season includes the Beastie Boys, the Hana Buttas, the Keanini Boys, the Hasegawa Generals and, yes, the Na-hiku Dinosaurs. High school basketball at the school gym also gets quite a large turnout and soccer is another fairly popular team sport. Hana afterall is just another small town entertaining itself.

Then there's canoeing. Everyday the Hana Canoe Club shows up at Hana Bay, hoist the outrigger and run it into the waves. If they're short a paddler, they'll recruit anyone on shore who is willing to fill in. Lots of fun. Very easy.

There are six paddlers in each canoe. The first paddler sets the speed. The second paddler signals when to change sides for the next series of strokes by shouting: "Hap Huli!" The second and fifth paddlers are responsible for bailing water out of the canoe, while the last paddler does the steering. This simple formula results in the beauty and grace of an outrigger gliding speedily and fluently along the surface of the water as the synchronized movement of the paddlers silhouette against the sky.

Many communities on each of the islands support a canoe club with their best rowers gathering for island wide competition and then for interisland competition.

(163) The Hana Canoe Club keeps the Hana section of the Hana Highway clean.

LIFE IN HANA

Then there is hunting and fishing which in Hana can hardly be considered as entertainment but rather as an opportunity to gather food.

There are some commercial fishing boats which go out each day with the day's catch sold to the local residents who come down to the Hana Bay pier when the boats come in. Some of the day's catch is sold to the Hana Hotel, the Hana Store or to Hasegawa's General Store.

I went fishing a couple of times with a friend who didn't know too much about fishing (though a whole lot more than I did). One time we stood on a rocky cliff at Wai-'anapanapa State Park located just before Hana town and caught quite a few varieties: several small 'elua, a few parrot fish and a couple of eels (which tasted somewhat like chicken when cooked).

The other two times I went fishing we didn't catch a thing. This was discouraging enough that I decided never to go fishing again unless accompanied by an expert. With the proper education and relationship with the sea, I can't imagine any local resident of Hana going fishing and not returning with lots of fish everytime.

Once I watched a net fisherman out on the rocks past 'Ohe'o Gulch, standing for a very long time, motionless, not a muscle twitching, net poised, reading the waves, waiting, waiting, waiting. Then whoosh, the net was thrown. For a fleeting moment the net rested on the surface of the water before the lead sinkers pulled it downward into the ocean's depths. Again within moments, the fisherman was pulling up a heavy load filled with the generous bounty of the sea. Enough abundance to feed his family and some neighbors he might pass on his way home.

Hunting wild pig and wild goats seems to be just as easy. Instead of a fishing hook or net, the hunter has a rifle and knife. Instead of standing at the water's edge, the hunter climbs the

(164) Historical markers like this one can be seen all over the island bringing your awareness to significant locations. The historical marker uses the image of a feathered robed and feathered helmeted Hawaiian chief, or member of the ali'i (nobility), of olden times.

mountain. Catching a pig becomes a major family event with the young children each holding onto a leg while boiling water is poured on the skin as the hair is scraped off before the pig is butchered and cooked.

Having nothing to do, or nothing to want to do, seems to be a major problem among the Hana teenagers. Many of them biding their time waiting to graduate Hana High School so they can move away and be far from parental supervision. Or to move to where there are more variety of jobs being offered, where there are more people and more things to do. Those who do not feel the pull of the fast lane eventually find their niche in Hana working either for the Hana Hotel, Hana Ranch or for the county road maintenance crew.

For myself, and for many others, the entertainment in Hana is provided by the projects that we choose to become involved in. Gardening and house building are the ones I most prefer. For me these projects are ongoing and take forever to complete. Always another detail. Always another addition.

Now we have a roof over our heads, let's put up some walls. Now we have a house completed, let's install a hot tub with a gazebo and landscape it with exotic gingers, heliconias, dracenas, bromeliads and begonias. Tending to the needs of my vegetable garden is another delightful preoccupation.

Sometimes entertainment for me is sitting out on my deck watching the clouds go by.

(165) Hana Clouds.

(166) The oriental entrance to the Heavenly Hana Inn. One of the oldest and most intimate overnight accomodations in Hana town.

(167) The old bull and his young apprentices.

(168) (169) Hana Bay: family beach, fishing off the pier, the canoe club, Tutu's Snack Shop, Helene Hall for cultural events and a great place for lu'aus.

(170) The old Hana School is now used as a community center for Hana's youth club, various civic organizations and Maui Community College.

(171) The old Hana District Police Station and Courthouse, in operation from 1871-1978, is now part of the Hana Museum Cultural Center.

(172) This building was the original Hana Store and is now the laundry facility for the Hotel Hana-Maui.

(173) Downtown Hana: the Post Office on the corner, the bank is a few doors down. There's also a couple of real estate offices and a gift store.

(174) Wa-na-na-lua Church is a 150 years old. Begun in 1842, it took 20 years to complete. There's a Hawaiian language Bible near the altar.

(175) Saint Mary's church is built in the Roman style.

(176) The Hongwangji Buddhist Temple, 1940, once serviced a large oriental population of contract laborers during sugar plantation days.

(177) Mint condition 1946 Packard bus takes Hotel Hana-Maui guests to and from the Hana Airport.

(178) Individual hotel bungalows border the hotel putting green.

(179) Recently developed 'millionaire' cottages. Each with an ocean view.

(180) Main entrance to the Hotel Hana-Maui.

(181) Beware! Day Care Center ahead.

(182) Hana Day Care Center nestled safely at the foot of cloud covered Hale-a-kala.

(183) Hana Ball Park the scene of great athletic competitions, Aloha Day celebrations and the gathering of the masses to hear local politicians.

(184) July '93: 6 theft, 2 seat belt citations, 52 parking citations, 43 expired safety stickers., 4 major & 3 minor accidents & 240 incidents.

Hana Medical Center

(185) Founded in 1964 by Dr. Milton H. Howell

The Hana Medical Center really does listen to the heartbeat of Hana.

Founded by the good doctor, Milton H. Howell, M.D. in 1964, the Hana Medical Center has known every resident of Hana in the most intimate manner and has certainly seen a fair share of tourists for all kinds of accidents and illnesses.

Dr. Howell was Hana's doctor for twenty-four years, 1962 through 1986. Everyday he could be seen walking the half mile from his home to the clinic in the morning, back and forth at lunch time then home again after closing.

But small town clinics never really close and small town doctors are always on call. If the phone rings, the doctor is on his way. In his last years before retirement, Doctor Howell moved out of Hana and bought a house from the O'ahu Dillingham family. The house (Photo #204) was situated half way between Hana and 'Ohe'o Gulch, about a 15 minute drive to the clinic.

Dr. Howell has since retired from a life of tending to the ills of humanity and has left Maui and has taken up residence in the state of Washington. His successor, Dr. John C. Clark, remained in Hana for awhile and has been replaced by Dr. Michelle Taube. As Dr. Taube is still breast feeding her infant daughter, it is her husband who can be seen walking the half mile to the clinic each day as he pushes their daughter's stroller.

Like Dr. Howell and Dr. Clark, Dr. Taube, assisted by some wonderful nurses and her excellent staff, is a compassionate person and much appreciated by the community. Like her predecessors, she is from the same allopathic school of family medicine which can diagnose pathology and prescribe the latest drug to alleviate pain and hopefully facilitate a healing.

In contrast to the allopathic school of medicine, in treating infectious or degenerative diseases, I prefer the Chinese system of Acupuncture, or the equally refined science of Homeopathy. It is the belief of these systems that antibiotics for infectious diseases suppress symptoms to keep them under control and do not necessarily cure illnesses.

To cure an illness it is necessary to stimulate the immune system to do the job it was developed by Nature to do: fight infection and eliminate it from the body. Antibiotics, in a sense, bypass the immune system and mask the illness by driving it deeper into the more vulnerable organs of the body which eventually resurface in later years as more complex problems involving the more vital organs.

There are numerous examples that can be cited from my twenty plus years of experience with homeopathy, acupuncture, herbalogy, naturopathy, etc. For me it is these alternative approaches that are my first line of defense. If these approaches do not seem to be working, then and only as a last resort, would I seek out assistance from an allopathic physician. And thus far I haven't had to.

With the allopathic approach to medicine the human animal is seen as a conglomerate of parts mechanically interacting much like a machine of the Industrial Age. With this perception one approaches health as a mechanic trying to find what part needs fixing or replacing.

What is now being referred to as the alternative approach espoused by homeopathy, oriental medicine, naturopathy, etc. perceives the human being as a whole organism with each part effecting each other part. These holistic approaches understand that the human physiology is held together by a kind of 'bio-electricity' that in western cultures has been called 'spirit.' In Latin it is called 'pneuma,' in India, 'prana,' in China, 'chi,' in Japan, 'ki' and in Hawai'i, 'mana.'

It is this so-called 'bio-electricity' that is the spark that keeps the immune system operating optimally. Without this 'electricity,' or Vital Life Force, the human organism begins to decompose, decay and turn to dust.

Homeopathy, along with naturopathy, herbalogy, midwifery and other varieties of non-intrusive forms of the healing arts are again making a comeback after many years of fighting the monopoly of power acquired in the early 1900's by the American Medical Association in cahoots with allopathic medical schools and the burgeoning pharmaceutical companies.

The renewal of interest in these so-called alternative forms of healthcare is the result of a developing distrust with the often poor results obtained by the current medical establishment. Interest is also being sparked as the relationship of diet to health and the benefit of preventive medicine has come to the foreground of public awareness.

[To learn more about homeopathy and to receive a free brochure write: Homeopathic Educational Services, 2124 Kitteredge St., Berkeley, CA 94704, or call: (415) 649-0294]

And I, like many residents of Hana, appreciate allopathetic physicians for what they do best: fixing broken bones, cleaning wounds, performing surgical proceedures, and in Doctor Howell's case, catching babies.

The statistics read: Dr. Milton H. Howell delievered 514 babies in the twenty-four years he ran the Hana Medical Center. Like many residents of Hana, I am one of those who greatly appreciated Doctor Howell when it came to catching babies.

In 1978, when my wife was pregnant, we would have preferred a home birth. At the time, the two midwives who resided on Maui were both off island, so we decided that Dr. Howell would be the baby catcher of choice. And I am very grateful he was. As I stood at my wife's head, holding her hands, breathing in unison, I witnessed the miracle of birth. I watched as Dr. Howell deftly guided my son's head and then body out of the birth canal, untangled the cord loosely coiled around his neck and passed the baby to me. I then placed my son on his mother's breast as he looked up and smiled.

(186) The Hana Medical Center - a well used facility and a very hard working dedicated staff.

HASEGAWA'S GENERAL STORE

NEWS FLASH - AUGUST 1990: Hasegawa's General Store, operating at the same location since the early 1900's, burned to the ground. Arson is suspected as the Chevron Station was also torched and the one house in between these two establishments remained untouched. A substantial reward has been posted in exchange for any information leading to the apprehension of the arsonist.

Hasegawa's General Store was first opened in 1910 by two brothers whose contracts as laborers on the Hana Sugar Plantation were completed.

The sugar plantation thrived from the mid-1800's till World War II. Once the plantation was closed the population of Hana quickly dwindled from several thousand to a few hundred.

The Hasegawa brothers saw that the needs of the Oriental laborers were not being adequately catered to by the Hana Company Store.

Eventually the two brothers decided to return to Japan and left the store to one of their sons. Now the store is run by Harry, the third generation of Hasegawa.

Harry is the oldest of four sons and studied accounting at the University of Colorado. After living in Los Angeles for a year, he served in the army and eventually returned to Hana to run the family business.

Neil Hasegawa, the fourth generation, has now reached the age where he too has become active in the family business and is quickly learning all there is to know.

Harry's father, mother and wife are also often seen bustling about the store, stocking shelves, keeping the merchandise in order and helping at the cash registers.

Until a new store can be built, the Hana Hotel/Ranch/Land Company has given the owners of Hasegawa's General Store, the Hasegawa family, permission to renovate the old Hana Movie Theater which since 1974 had been used as a storage facility.

The use of the old movie theater has enabled the Hasegawa family to continue operating their business until the new store is built and thereby alleviate the burden on the Hana Store which is now having to handle all the needs of Hana and of the tourists passing through Hana town.

The landmark Hasegawa's General Store boasts as their slogan: "Far from Waikiki." Though groceries are offered as well as gas (diesel, regular and unleaded), the primary business is making available to Hana residents everything one could possibly imagine. Under the Hasegawa roof you can find everything from nuts and bolts to replacement parts for kerosene lanterns. You can find pots and pans, lumber, plumbing fixtures and compost for the garden. Plus, video rentals, fishing supplies and ice for the cooler.

Hasegawa's General Store

You name it and it is probably available at Hasegawa's General Store. Pareus, machetes, straw hats, toys, camping supplies, fan belts, medicinals, magazines, stationery, film, etc. etc. etc. The place is packed with stuff.

Sometimes you can even find a bargain as an item might be cheaper at Hasegawa's if it had been there long enough for prices to go up elsewhere.

Hasegawa's is also the UPS drop-off, has a Fax service, a one hour photo developing service and an ATM for cash withdrawals.

One always feels the "alo-ha" of those who work at Hasegawa's. Whether keeping the produce looking good, pumping gas out front or helping at the check-out counter, the employees at Hasegawa's have always been courteous, friendly and efficient.

And Harry Hasegawa himself seems always available to answer questions or give advice on the best way to repair or fix whatever your problem might be.

Over the years, Hasegawa's General Store and its bustling activity has become another Hana tourist attraction. Everyone in Hana was glad when Hasegawa's re-opened in the old movie theater and the many services that Hasegawa's provided were again available.

(187) Hasegawa's General Store as it looked before it burned to the ground. Behind this unassuming facade was a major supply house for everything needed by the residents and visitors to Hana. Hasegawa's motto was: "Far from Waikiki."

(188) After the fire destroyed the original General Store, Hasegawa moved into the old Hana Movie Theater, closed since 1974. In no time, business was as usual. Eventually a new store will be built on the lot where the old store used to stand. Rumor has it that the new store will have a restaurant on the second floor with an ocean view.

(189) A towering mix of Cook and Norfolk Island Pines lead you out of Hana as you begin the long drive to 'Ohe'o Gulch, Ki-pahulu and beyond.

(190) Two friendly gods greet guests at this Hana residence situated down at the ocean's edge.

(191) Hana Ranch horses graze in Maka-'alae, ignoring the approaching rain storm. In Hana it can rain for days without one sunny day.

(192) Winter time and the beach at Koki is covered with water and offers little sun shine for sun bathers. Still a fun place to play.

(193) Alau Island with two palm trees. Some say, two starcross lovers. Some say, two who died in war. Shige says, he and his dad planted them.

(194) Fish ponds like this were part of old Hawaiian aquaculture. Fish come over the man made reef and stay to be caught as the tide ebbs.

(195) White sand Ha-mou Beach is opened to the public but is maintained with beach chairs, umbrellas and facilities by the Hotel Hana-Maui.

(196) Typical green or red stained cane workers house with tin roof slopping in all four directions.

(197) Gazebo on a million dollar ocean front property.

(198) Cemetery at St. Peter's Roman Catholic Church, built in 1859 on Pu'u-iki Hill.

(199) After this sign the Road gets bumpier and less comfortable to travel.

(200) These carved pigs have slowed traffic down for over twenty years.

(201) Helio's Cross as seen through the twisted branches of the Monkey Pod tree. Helio, a Hawaiian, brought Catholicism to this side of Maui.

(202) 'Ohe'o Gulch in the distance. One of the last Hawaiian villages on this side of the island was located on the beach in the right foreground.

(203) The Road to the Seven Pools continually gets worse.

(204) The house Dr. Howell purchased from the Dillingham family. The last house with electricity. The rest use propane, solar power or generators.

(205) 95 foot Wai-lua Waterfall at Wai-lua Bridge cascades off rock ledges.

(206) Wai-lua Bridge is last major tourist attraction before the Seven Pools.

(207) Ku-kui, or Candlenut, forest. The nuts were strung together with a wick. The wick was lit and the nuts burned for quite a few hours.

(208) Just another narrow bridge through the jungle thicket.

(209) The Road continues to disappear around seemingly endless twists and curves.

(210) Grotto with a stone Virgin Mary is always festooned with exotic flowers and garlands.

'OHE'O GULCH & THE SEVEN POOLS

It has been said that the Hana Highway doesn't go anywhere. That Hana or 'Ohe'o Gulch are merely locations along the Road and serve as convenient turn around places. In other words, the Hana Highway itself is the destination.

True, the waterfalls and pools along 'Ohe'o Stream are beautiful and certainly worth the drive for those who are hale and hearty and who love adventure. There are excellent camping facilities in a pasture on a bluff overlooking the ocean. And no permits are needed in National Parks. Just show up and pitch a tent. Recently, composting toilets have been installed making the campers' and other park visitors' lives a little more civilized.

Tents are recommended as you are almost guaranteed to get rained on during the night. Rainfall at 'Ohe'o and in Ki-pahulu is almost 60 inches per year less than in Hana town. But even 80 inches a year is rainy enough to keep the pastures velvety green and the rest of the scenery quite lush.

For those who spend the night at the camp grounds the morning brings a most remarkable reward. The ocean, the sky, the land, they all dance together herein the most magical way. The beauty of this location is breath taking. It is easy to sit silently here for quite some time absorbing the charged up atmosphere. White clouds, blue sky, ocean surging. This is a place to refill and feel renewed. No one who comes here ever wants to leave. Everyone who comes here vows to return.

Meandering across the pasture under the hala trees from the camp grounds to the lower pools for an early morning swim in the early morning light is to find paradise unsullied for a fleeting moment in the spectrum of time.

(211) 'Ohe'o Gulch was added to the National Park Service in 1969.

(212) Sound Horn on this narrow hairpin turn.

90 * THE NARROW WINDING ROAD

(213) 'Ohe'o Gulch - looking toward the ocean. On the bridge is a red 'X' marking the spot for the safest place to dive.

(214) 'Ohe'o Gulch - looking up the stream at the cascading waterfalls and pools.

(215) The three mile hike to 400 foot high Wai-moku Falls begins here in this cow pasture.

(216) This gate leads you from the cow pastures to the jungle trail that takes you through the bamboo forest to Wai-moku Falls.

(217) There are two spots to dive from into the pool below, one at 30 feet, the other at 25 feet.

(218) Jumping from rock to rock to cross 'Ohe'o Stream.. Do not try to cross this stream when it's raining heavily.

'Ohe'o Gulch & The Seven Pools

But for the tourists planning on a dash out and a dash back again, 'Ohe'o Gulch really doesn't offer much more than just a convenient turn around. For the individual who is prepared to camp out, or who has a vacation rental or hotel room in Hana, then 'Ohe'o Gulch and Hale-a-kala National Park offer some of the best hiking trails on Maui along with an experience of one of the most beautiful places in the world.

Much of the land along 'Ohe'o Gulch and extending up through a major portion of Ki-pahulu Valley to the rim of Hale-a-kala was purchased by the Nature Conservancy and added to the Hale-a-kala National Park in 1969. This was done in an attempt to preserve this area's unique character and the many rare species and ecosystems that exist here.

The Baldwin Family once owned almost all the land along the south shore stretching from Ulu-pala-kua to Ki-pahulu. The land comprising the Ki-pahulu Ranch also included 'Ohe'o Gulch and the Seven Pools.

When the Baldwin Family decided to sell these properties, Laurence Rockefeller purchased fifty-two acres around the Seven Pools in an attempt to keep the land from hotel developers until transfer could be made to the National Park Service.

Below the bridge that crosses 'Ohe'o Gulch are the pools which are so heavily promoted in travel brochures. Which is why people often ask the question when reaching Hana town: "Where are the Seven Sacred Pools?" Or, "How much further to the Seven Sacred Pools?" Followed by, "Is it worth the drive?"

The real answer to this perennial question, "Where are the Seven Sacred Pools?" is, "There is no such place."

The name, Seven Sacred Pools, was literally an invention of the tourist industry. Apparently, the name was first used either by the local Hana Hotel or by a rent-a-car company as a publicity gimmick to get people to go on a long drive to what was considered at that time to be out to nowhere.

Nevertheless, by the 1970's, almost everyone was using the designation, The Seven Sacred Pools, to refer to the beautiful pools and cascading waterfalls of 'Ohe'o Stream.

By 1979, all state agencies eliminated this false advertising from their information literature and most map makers and guidebooks were, or should have been, updated using the proper designation of 'Ohe'o Stream. Though many people still refer to this area as the Seven Pools dropping the reference to Sacred.

By the late 1970's, as more people chose Maui as their vacation destination, more people headed for what were being called the Seven Pools as a beautiful place to see. As the number of cars to the Pools multiplied, it became necessary to restrict the parking near the bridge and build a parking lot to accommodate the influx of sightseers.

There used to be only two or three park rangers keeping watch at the bridge. When I lived in Ki-pahulu, I used to jog down to the bridge crossing 'Ohe'o Gulch each morning and 'talk story' with whichever ranger was on duty and after a while, jog home again.

Needless to say, as the Pools be-

(219) On the way to Wai-moku Falls you pass smaller waterfalls, 200 ft. Maka-hiku Falls.

(220) Entering the giant bamboo forest. Bamboo leaves among the lava rocks.

(221) Walking through the bamboo forest. As you look up, it is impossible to see the sky.

'OHE'O GULCH & THE SEVEN POOLS

came busy with people, it became necessary to hire additional helpers. It appears that the job performed by the park rangers is primarily that of traffic monitors. Another job of the park rangers is that of first-aiders. Unfortunately, the rangers are often seen grabbing the stretcher and rushing off to rescue some hapless individual who slipped on the rocks. They'll even help you open your car door if you happened to lock your car keys inside. Everyone agrees,

(222) (223) (224) Coming out of the bamboo forest, you see 400 foot high Wai-moku Falls. "To be at Wai-moku Falls can have an almost cathedral-like quality."

'Ohe'o Gulch & The Seven Pools

they're a great bunch of guys.

For those who get out to 'Ohe'o Gulch early, there is the additional opportunity to hike the four miles up to Wai-moku Falls. Wai-moku Falls is 400 feet high and one of the highest waterfalls on Maui. The highest is 1,120 foot high Hono-ko-hau waterfall which is located in the West Maui Mountains.

The hike to Wai-moku Falls begins with a walk up hill through cow pastures. Next, you go across the stream which is easy to cross if it is not swollen by heavy rains. The first time I hiked this trail, my friend and I had to swim to the other side. We also had to come back down before the next flash flood would make crossing the stream a total impossibility.

Once on the other side of the stream, you go up a short hill to a trail which goes through a dark and musty bamboo forest. As you wander through this forest, you hear the knocking of bamboo poles against each other like a giant bamboo wind chime. Except this wind chime is made up of thousands of bamboo poles towering above you. As you look up, it is impossible to see the sky.

After you come out of the bamboo forest, you continue along a jungle trail and then enter another stretch of dense bamboo. Finally, the trail takes you through jungle growth along the 'Ohe'o Stream where you can see exotic bird's nest ferns perched high in the branches of the le'hua trees. It is not to much further before you see the magnificent Wai-moku Falls, and not too much further before you are standing at the pool looking up and feeling the spray of water as it comes crashing down.

If you get there early enough, before 9 a.m. you will be able to enjoy this peaceful, serene location without the distraction of any other people. In the old days, any day, any hour, it was possible to sit alone at Wai-moku Falls and imbibe the super electrified oxygen ions. To feel the 'power,' the 'mana' or Vital Life Force, flowing through the top of your head and up and down your spine. To be at Wai-moku Falls can have almost a cathedral-like religious quality.

On the way down, after the bamboo forest, as you re-cross the stream, if you are a thrill seeker and a good swimmer (and there are no high water warnings), you may want to consider diving off the cliff into the pool below.

There are two spots to dive from: one at thirty feet and one at twenty-five feet. Once in the pool below the only way out is by sliding down the lava to the next pool below it.

Next you have to swim the length of that pool and again slide carefully down to the next pool below that one. As you swim to the other side of that pool, you can then walk ashore, follow the trail through the guava trees and connect back to the main trail that takes you down the mountain back to the parking lot and back to the Hana Highway.

(225) *Monkey Pod Tree silhouetted by the sun.*

(226) *"The trail takes you through jungle growth...where you can see exotic bird's nest ferns perched high in the branches of the le'hua trees."*

(227) *The tops of bamboo tower overhead.*

(228) *"To feel the power, the 'mana' or Vital Life Force, flowing through the top of your head and up and down your spine."*

Ki-pahulu

In the last few years, Mike Love of the popular rock group, The Beach Boys, has purchased some fabulous ocean front property past 'Ohe'o Gulch down the Ki-pahulu Road.

His initial land acquisition was previously owned by Sam Pryor (no relation to comedian Richard Pryor who in more recent years bought and then sold a nice piece of property in the Ka-'eleku subdivision near the Hana Airport).

Sam Pryor had purchased the land from the Baldwin Family, who, as mentioned, owned almost all of Ki-pahulu. Apparently, he had been given the option to purchase the land surrounding the Seven Pools, but refrained when he realized how his ownership would conflict with public usage. So he chose instead a more secluded jungle location with less frequented waterfalls, pools and ocean access. Ownership of some of this land, as with other lands around the state, has recently come up for legal dispute as to the questionable means by which title was claimed.

(229) The Ki-pahulu portion of the Road starts here where the paved road used to end. Sign says, ROUGH ROAD - NEXT 7 MILES.

In attempt to preserve Ki-pahulu's jungle wilderness beauty, Rockefeller, Pryor, the new owners of the Ki-pahulu Ranch and other wealthy Ki-pahulu property owners made an agreement that they would each build their houses out of view of each other. They also refused to sign the right of way documents requested by the electric company. This kept the electric company from erecting power lines through this area.

I met old Sam Pryor after he had already been retired as a vice-president of the now defunct Pan Am World Airlines. In addition to his status as head of one of the world's largest airlines, he had also gained notoriety as a key player in the Interpol (International Police) drug bust which became known to the public as the book and movie titled, The French Connection.

Sam was quite an eccentric character who raised two gibbon apes whom he treated like his children. During the time I lived in the guest house on the Charles and Anne Morrow Lindbergh property, which was next to Sam Pryor's estate, I witnessed the voracious appetite of Sam's baby girl monkey as she escaped from her cage one day and came swinging through our opened window.

The baby girl monkey sat on our stalk of bananas and proceeded to take one bite out of each banana before tossing it aside. It was a very graphic portrayal of the competition that would eventually ensue between fruit eating monkeys and fruit eating humans if the monkeys ever went wild on the islands of Hawai'i. After Sam Pryor died, the apes became residents of the Maui Zoo in Ka-hu-lui.

It is also Sam Pryor who allegedly is responsible for the infestation of the large red ants that are seen everywhere in Ki-pahulu. Apparently he imported a plant that did not go through the proper agricultural clearance.

Charles Lindbergh moved to Ki-pahulu on the encouragement of his friend, the just mentioned Pan Am executive, Sam Pryor. Charles Lindbergh and his wife, Anne Morrow, came to Ki-pahulu to escape his "pilot of the Spirit of St. Louis's fame," the publicity of the infamous kidnapping and still unsolved disappearance and suspected murder of their child from their home in New Jersey and some of the negative attention he received after he publicly endorsed Adolf Hitler, Nazism and the belief in Aryan genetic superiority. He was actually moving to Berlin when the war broke out.

(230) The Ki-pahulu church where aviator Charles Lindbergh is buried.

I arrived on Maui, in October 1974, which was just after the much celebrated aviator had died of lung cancer the previous August. There was a small write-up in Time and Newsweek magazines about his home in Ki-pahulu.

In the same articles it was also mentioned that Charles Lindbergh was buried in an unmarked grave at the Old Ki-pahulu Church, the Pala-pala Ho'omau Congregational Church built in 1848. His gravesite was unmarked so "it would not be disturbed by those who still worshipped him as a hero." But this did not deflect the numerous tourists who came to Ki-pahulu to stand by their hero's grave and pay homage to the famous man.

Needless to say, the graveyard at the Old Ki-pahulu Church was soon overrun by individuals wanting to pay their last respects to Charles Lindbergh. At that time the Lindbergh gravesite was a more popular tourist destination than 'Ohe'o Stream which had just begun being called the Seven Sacred Pools.

Eventually, the destruction of the other gravesites neighboring Lindbergh's grave necessitated placing a gravemarker on Charles Lindbergh's final resting place (Photos #232 & #233).

Often people came down my driveway, camera in hand, asking if I knew where the Lindbergh house was. The Lindbergh driveway, like the Charles Lindbergh gravesite, was unmarked. "Yes, I do," I would say, "but let's respect the Lindbergh family's desire for privacy. Enjoy the Seven Pools and your drive home. Alo-ha."

In 1975, I lived in the Lindbergh's rented guest house briefly. The main room was completely enclosed by sliding glass windows and the house itself was situated on a bluff overlooking a black sand beach. When the Sun rose each dawn, the sky turned golden. On the adjacent property was an abandoned papaya orchard and all around there was great abundance of various varieties of buttery avocados, tasty bananas, sweet and juicy mangos, nourishing coconuts and much more. At times I truly felt that I was actually in the Garden of Eden, that I had found Paradise.

The trail from the guest cottage to the black sand beach passed in front of the main house. One time, as I was coming back up the cliff from the black sand beach below with my arms full of driftwood I had gathered, Anne Morrow came rushing across the lawn nervously asking what I was going to do with all that driftwood.

I replied that I was going to build a mobile for one of the neighbors.

She gave a 'sigh of relief' and in her frail voice said, "Oh, that's all right then. I was concerned that perhaps you were going to use the driftwood to make a fire and you know that driftwood had been polished by the sea for hundreds of years. It is very special. I'm sure your mobile will also be as special."

Anne Morrow Lindbergh is the author of the much read naturalist classic, Gift From the Sea, published in 1955. She now lives on an island off the coast of Florida.

The family decided there was no longer any reason to hold on to their Ki-pahulu property. As soon as it went up for sale, Mike Love of The Beach Boys gobbled the five acres up for a cool one million.

Property values all over Maui have sky rocketed over the years. Now, in the 1990's, undeveloped land starts at $20,000 to $50,000 and I know of a one beautiful ocean front acre with the asking price of one million!

And last but not least there's the Butterfly Mailbox.

(231) Believe me, along with the heart there is also a butterfly on this mailbox.

(232) Charles Lindbergh's grave is in the foreground. The Pala-pala Ho'omau Congregational Church in the background.

(233) Charles Lindbergh's tombstone inscribed: "If I take the wings of the morning and dwell in the uttermost parts of the sea."

(234) On the ocean side wall of the church is an Hawaiian Jesus painted on glass wearing the traditional feather robe of the Ali'i (chiefs).

LEAVING HANA-SIDE

And now it's time to return to wherever you came from. There are only two ways to go. You can either continue past Ki-pahulu around the backside of the island on the Old Pi'i-lani Highway or Kau-po Road, or return the way you came.

If you choose to take the Kau-po Road back to the Other Side you will find that after the dirt road through Ki-pahulu, the Road gets even rougher for the first five miles of the Kau-po Road. There are quite a few additional bridges to cross and three riverbeds which are usually dry. The scenery is awesome but be watchful as you drive the backside of the island as it is open grazing and you are likely to encounter several cows walking on the Road.

Or, you can go back the way you came, back along the twists and turns of the Hana Highway, all the way back to the Other Side.

Or perhaps you would rather stay in Hana and watch the clouds go by.

Alo-ha ——

(235) More Hana clouds.

102 * THE NARROW WINDING ROAD

CHANGES SINCE I BEGAN THIS BOOK

1. Car tires were removed (Photo #16) in the fall of 1990.

2. The Stop Sign in Pa'ia (Photo #21) has been replaced with a traffic light.

3. The NARROW WINDING ROAD (Photo #30) and other older road signs (Photo #153) were replaced with newer signs having reflector borders.

4. Mayor Linda Crockett Lingle in June 1992 came out in favor of lengthening the Ka-hu-lui Airport runway to encourage international flights (page 15).

5. One of the One Way signs (Photo #74) at Pu-a'a Ka'a State Wayside Park had been knocked down and then removed.

6. In a recent investigation, not yet made public, it has been alledged that EMI, (the East Maui Irrigation Company owned and operated by the Alexander and Baldwin Company), only has the legal rights to 5% of the water it takes from the water runoffs that extend along the coast to the Seven Pools/'Ohe'o Gulch area (Page 30). If this is true then EMI owes the people of Maui County and the State of Hawai'i approximately $20 million dollars a year for agricultural water use since it began diverting water for their own profit making ventures.

7. Colin C. Cameron, 69, (Page 32) the head of Maui Land and Pineapple Company died of an apparent heart attack June 1992.

8. The mountain side (Photo #88) was removed in 1993 to minimize accidents from landslides.

9. The State okayed the operation of the Puna Geothermal well in October 1992. This is one year behind schedule due to blowouts and court decisions.

10. John, the palm frond weaver (Photos #106-108), is no longer in Ke-'anae. He now has a table in Hana at the entrance to Helani Gardens just past Mile Marker #33.

11. Aloha Donny (Photo #113) sold his tour van company and is now Wally the Whaler.

12. The Na-pili 'A' Well servicing La-haina was closed March 21, 1992 due to "unacceptable levels of the pesticide DBCP." The pesticide DBCP, a known carcinogen, was being used in the neighboring pineapple fields (Page 52).

13. Rastabro John sold his car (Photo #150) and moved to the Big Island.

14. The school gym (Photo #159) now has a fancy paved parking lot and driveway.

15. The Road from Ha-moa to 'Ohe'o (Photo #203) was paved May-July 1992. The Kipahulu Road (Photo #229) was also paved in 1992. This encourages tourists to use the road through Kaupo and around the backside of the island alleviating the burden on the Hana Coast Road and increasing the burden on the Old Pi'ilani Highway.

16. The weed covered car (Photo #240) disappeared one day in 1992. Most have been hauled off to the dump.

17. The graffitti on the wall (Photo #250) has been covered by shrubbery.

18. On September 7, 1993, after a long legal debate, the Maui County Council approved the Hotel Hana-Maui's bid to build a golf course with a 1,500 foot buffer instead of the 300 foot buffer requested. This curtails plans to build executive mansions on the 770 acres around the golf course. The Japanese owner, Ted Kato, (51% of the HanaHotel/Ranch/Land Company called Keola Hana Maui), was hoping to pay debts and build the golf course with golf course memberships of $200,000 each to be sold on the Japanese Commodities Market. Recent changes in Japanese law forbids sale of memberships before golf courses are actually built. Now the Hotel is looking for other ways to finance this controversial project.

BIBLIOGRAPHY

Cooper, George and Gaven Daws. **LAND AND POWER IN HAWAII: The Democratic Years.** Honolulu: Benchmark Books, 1985.

Daws, Gavan. **THE SHOALS OF TIME: A History of the Hawaiian Islands.** Honolulu: Univ. of Hawaii Press, 1968.

Fuchs, Lawrence H. **HAWAII PONO: A Social History**. NYC: Harcourt Brace & World, 1961.

Harden, M.J. **MAGIC MAUI, The Best of the Island, 3rd Ed.** Wailuku: Aka Press, 1988.

Jensen, Lucia Tarallo and Rocky. **MEN OF ANCIENT HAWAII.** Anima Gemella Co., 1975.

Lee, Pali Jae and Koko Willis. **TALES OF THE NIGHT RAINBOW.** Honolulu: Night Rainbow Publ. Co.,1990.

Long, Max Freedom. **THE SECRET SCIENCE BEHIND MIRACLES.** M. D. Rey, CA: DeVorss & Co., 1950.

Morrow, Ann. **GIFTS FROM THE SEA.** N.Y.: Vintage Books, 1975.

Rayson, Ann. **MODERN HAWAIIAN HISTORY.** Honolulu: Bess Press, 1984.

Wenkam, Robert. **MAUI: THE LAST HAWAIIAN PLACE.** N.Y.: Friends of the Earth, 1970.

Wisniewski, Richard A. **HAWAII THE TERRITORIAL YEARS 1900 -1959.** Honolulu: Pacific Basin Enterprises, 1984.

Youngblood, Ron with contributions from Creamer, Lindquist & Wong. **ON THE HANA COAST.** Honolulu: Emphasis International & Lindquist, 1983.

ABOUT THE AUTHOR

Shave Ice Solomon is a pseudonym for a Hana resident who appreciates anonimity and the special opportunity that living on the Hana side of Maui offers for those who enjoy Silence and Retreat.

Thank you for buying this book and allowing me to share with you my love for the Hana Highway and the Hana side of the island of Maui.

Mahalo & Aloha, Shave Ice Solomon

(236) The author on the Road again.

(237) (238) (239) (240) CARS LEFT IN THE JUNGLE TOO LONG: Eventually the jungle devours anything and everything, even metal. Here are some cars that were parked in one place too long.

Special Resource Directory

SHAVE ICE SOLOMON'S
REVIEWS

Hana: Where To Stay & What To Do
Pa'ia: Our Favorite Places
Ka-hului: Back To The Beginning
Other Wonderful Maui Things To Do

HANA: WHERE TO STAY & WHAT TO DO

PLACES TO STAY

Hotel Hana-Maui: This world class hotel offers a wide variety of accommodations from private bungalows overlooking the sea (Photo #179) to smaller units within the main hotel facility. The hotel offers a putting green (Photo #178), horseback riding, a Wellness Center featuring an outdoor swimming pool, a complete gymnasium and well trained massage therapists. In the hotel's main facility there is fine dining, gift shops, an art gallery, fashion clothing store, a convenience store and a beauty parlor.

The original hotel was built in the 1940's as the home of Paul and Helene Fagan. It is the Fagan's who converted the old sugar plantation into the Hana Ranch. It soon became obvious that their home needed to be remodeled in order to accommodate the many guests who wanted to visit the Fagan's in beautiful Hana. Soon Hana became a resort destination for the rich and famous. The hotel picks up visitors at the Hana Airport in a mint condition 1946 Packard bus (Photo #177). It also uses this bus to take hotel guests to the hotel maintained Hamoa Beach (Photo #195). Call 248-8211 or 1-800-321-4262.

Heavenly Hana Inn: (Photo #166) This Hana landmark is situated at the very beginning of Hana town on the makai (ocean) side immediately after the Hana High and Elementary School. The Heavenly Hana offers several very private rooms all with pleasant garden views. The design is oriental and the environment serene. 248-8442.

Hana Plantation Houses: Situated in various locations around Hana town and out toward the Seven Pools, these vacation rentals come with everything to make a stay in Hana really comfortable. Some facilities have hot tubs and some are in walking distance to Hana Bay. 248-7248 or 1-800-657-7723.

Hana Ali'i Holidays: Another excellent way to enjoy an extended stay in Hana town. The Hana Ali'i has grown over the years to include various vacation rentals in the Hana area. In addition to its one bedroom units overlooking picturesque Hana Bay, there are also cottages and homes located in different unique settings around the Hana area. Rates start at a reasonable $60 a night. 248-7742 or 1-800-548-0478.

Hana Kai - Maui Resort: Until recently, the Hotel Hana-Maui, Heavenly Hana Inn and the Hana Kai were the only accommodations available in Hana town. And only the Hana Kai was situated on Hana Bay with its own little black sand beach. At the Hana Kai you can still rent limited service, first class studio and one bedroom condo units on the water. Member AAA. 248-8426, 248-7506 or 1-800-346-2772.

Hana Hou Hale: These three recently built units with a great view of Hana Bay can be rented individually or to accommodate a large group. They are located on Ua'kea Road just above Hana Bay. Hana Hou Hale is equipped for every need with the main two bedroom unit featuring a jacuzzi tub and spa. 248-7067.

Aloha Cottage: Many of my friends have stayed at these comfortable units in the center of Hana town on Ke-awa Street across from the Hotel Hana-Maui's putting green and steps away from Hana Bay (Photo #168-169). The owners are very gracious and Mrs. Nakamura might even help you fillet a fresh caught fish. 248-8420.

Joe's Place: As you come to the Medical Center and the fork in the road at the Police Station, take Ua'kea, the low road, to Joe's Place. You can't miss it, as Joe has signs up in several places. Rooms are inexpensive with the kitchen and T.V. room open to all guests. Perfect for those on a low budget. This place is real down home. 248-7033.

Wai-'anapanapa State Park: There are several cabins with bunk beds, kitchen and shower at $15 a night. Great place to stay and understandably a long waiting list. Best bet is to make arrangements well in advance. At another end of the park there is an area for tenting near the park restrooms and outside shower (Photo #154-#156). Wai-'anapanapa State Park is located just after Mile Marker #32 on the ma-kai side of the Hana Highway and before the Hana High and Elementary School. Call the State Department of Parks in Wai-lu-ku for permits to camp or for availability of the cabins. 244-4354.

'Ohe'o Gulch/Seven Pools: Unlike Wai-'anapanapa State Park which requires camping permits, the National Park Service does not require permits to use their camping facility. Hale-a-kala National Park (Photos #211-#228) is a half hour drive further down the Hana Highway past Hana town. If you really like camping out, have an adequate tent, camp stove and food. If it doesn't rain, you'll want to stay for as long as you can.

PLACES TO EAT

Hotel Hana-Maui Restaurant: The Hotel restaurant serves excellent cuisine exquisitely prepared featuring many traditional Hawaiian preparations. The restaurant is open only to Hotel guests except during certain hours when 'outsiders' are seated. Reservations are necessary.

Hana Ranch Restaurant & Take-Out: (Photo #162) in the Hana Town Center prepares sandwiches and plate lunches to go. My favorite take-out: the grilled ahi special with fries. Inside is a lunch buffet while Friday and Saturday nights the restaurant opens for dinner. Sometimes there's evening entertainment and Thursday is Pizza Night.

Tutu's Snack Shop: at Hana Bay. Tutu's is the place to go for local favorites like Teriyaki Burgers, grilled hot dogs or Avo and Veggie Sandwiches. Open for breakfast and lunch.

Hana Gardenland Cafe & Expresso Bar: The 'in' place to go for sandwiches, snacks, fresh fruit smoothies and juices prepared with your health in mind. Located after Mile Marker #31 on the corner of Kalo Road and the Hana Highway. 248-7340.

Hasegawa's General Store on the Hana Highway (pages 108-109, Photos #187 & #188) and **Hana Store** (in the Hana Town Center): both of these markets situated in the center of Hana have beverages, pre-made lunches, canned foods, fresh vegetables and other snacks.

Roadside Fruit Stands: All along the Hana Highway and on some of the side roads are roadside fruit stands. Most of these fruit stands are operated on an honor system with the price marked on the offered fruits and a jar for you to deposit your change (Photos #144 & #146). Flowers, flower leis and other items may also be for sale. Prices are good (very low overhead) and usually helps some kid earn pocket money for his or her endeavors.

Hana: Where To Stay & What To Do

POINTS OF INTEREST

Wai-'anapanapa State Park: A beautiful black sand beach, the Queen's Cave, a blow hole and awesome coastline nature walks already described on page 66 (Photos #154-156).

King's Highway: begins at Wai-'anapanapa's black sand beach. This ancient footpath meanders along a lava rock cliff pass an ancient heiau (temple) all the way to Hana town.

Hana Cultural Center & Historical Hana District Courthouse: (Photo #171) Here you can glimpse Hana and Hawai'i's past through a wonderful exhibit of old photographs and artifacts. The center is situated on the mau-ka side of Ua'kea Street (the low road) past the Hana Police Station, pass Joe's Place and just before Hana Bay. 248-8622.

Hana Bay: (Photos #168 & #169) Quiet and peaceful Hana Bay is a place for the whole family. Safe waters for children, a ramp for launching boats and plenty of space for lu'aus. It is the home of the Hana Canoe Club, Tutu's Snack Shop and Helene Hall for special events, classes, dances and other public activities like vehicle registration. There is a public telephone, outdooor shower and changing cabana. Hana Bay has it all.

Fagan's Memorial: (Photo #161) Opposite the entrance of the Hotel Hana-Maui up Lyon's Hill is a 30 foot cross made of blocks carved from lava rock erected in the memory of Paul Fagan, the founder of the Hana Ranch. It's a short hike up the hill with a great view of Hana Bay and Hana town.

Jogging & Hiking Trail: Further up the path from Fagan's Cross is a two and a half mile cinder track laid over the narrow gauge rails of the old plantation railway tracks. The views are spectacular and the exercise environment great.

Wa-na-na-lua Church: This church on the corner of Hau'oli Street and the Hana Highway was built in 1842 from lava blocks and coral cement (Photo #174). There is a rare Hawaiian language Bible near the altar.

Hongwangji Buddhist Temple: (Photo #176) This historic temple once served a large oriental population during sugar plantation days. It was recently restored as a community effort funded by corporations, individuals and Hawai'i Buddhist organizations throughout the State of Hawai'i.

Koki & Hamoa Beaches: (Photos #192 & #195) Less than a mile out of Hana town is a detour off the Hana Highway on the left that goes down Haneo'o Road to Koki and then Hamoa Beach. Here you will find Hana's only white sand beaches with waves that are excellent for body and board surfing.

BOTANICAL GARDENS

Ali'i Gardens: One of the largest commercial flower farms on Maui providing exotic flowers for shipment to markets around the world. Ali'i Gardens are located on 55 acres in Upper Na-hiku after Mile Marker #26 (Photo #141). The gardens are open to the public Monday through Friday, 7am to 4pm. 248-7217.

HANA: WHERE TO STAY & WHAT TO DO

Hana Gardenland: Located at Mile Marker #31 just pass Hau'oli Lio Stables on the corner of Kalo Road, Hana Gardenland is the oldest certified export nursery on Maui, shipping orchids, anthuriums and exotic plants worldwide. Originally owned by the Sanders family, Hana Gardenland has been beautifully restored by the owners of Plantation House Vacation Rentals. In addition to the five acres of exotic ornamentals, Hana Gardenland has an art gallery, juice bar and cafe. 248-8975.

THINGS TO DO

Hau'oli Lio Riding Stables: Arrangements for mountain rides can be made by calling Hana Ali'i Holidays at their main office. 248-7742.

Hana Hou Charters: The owners of Hana Hou Hale also provide fishing, snorkeling or any other scenic tour or ocean activity aboard their Coast Guard certified vessel. 248-7067.

'Ohe'o Stables: Experience guides will take you on riding trails high in the tropical rainforests above the Seven Pools. Magnificent views. 667-2222.

SERVICES AVAILABLE

Hana Tresures: Here you can find Hana designed T-Shirts, gifts, jewelry and Hawaiian memorabilia. Located in the Hana Town Center across from the Hana Ranch Restaurant. 248-7372.

Hana Ranch Trading Company: A place to find gifts and fine apparel for men, women and children. Located at the Hotel Hana-Maui. 248-8298.

Hana Coast Gallery: Many fine artists and craftspeople from the islands are featured here including Hana's own Thomas Booth, Karen Davidson, Joyce Clark, Stan Ort, Winn Redmond, Carla Crow, Diana Lehr, Bill and Maria Love and Mia Parry. Hana Coast Gallery is also located at the Hotel Hana-Maui. 248-8636.

The Hana News: Edited by Alberta deJetley since 1991, the Hana News is the only source for local news of Hana, Maui. Articles might include such controversial topics as whether or not the Hotel Hana-Maui can put in an 18 hole golf course or where to locate affordable housing. Along with news concerning healthcare and education, there is the usual small town news about retirments, anniversaries and graduations. To subscribe or advertise call 248-7093.

The Salon: Dot Pua is the lady to see for any style and any cut. She is located in the Hotel Hana-Maui and is available by appointment only. 248-8211, x146.

Massage Therapy: Ramaia Collins (Lic. #MAT 1580) has provided relief for Hana residents and visitors alike. He specializes in deep tissue work and has relieved many backaches. 248-7075.

TRANSPORTATION

Dollar Rent-A-Car: The Hana office is located across from the Heavenly Hana Inn. 248-8237.

Air Molokai: If you aren't thrilled with the long and winding road to Hana, then consider flying. Air Moloka'i has scheduled service connecting Ka-hu-lui Airport to Hana and transports you in one of its nine passenger Cessna 402 twin engine aircraft. A great fifteen minute ride at a great price. Reservations and flight times: 877-0026.

PA'IA - OUR FAVORITE PLACES

I've always enjoyed the small town character of Pa'ia and its old wooden facades, reminders of its days as a bustling sugar cane town teeming with the new immigrants from the Phillipines and the Orient.

Today Pa'ia's character is more mixed than in former plantation days since the influx of ha-ole youths in the sixties and early seventies. The ha-oles of Pa'ia used to be referred to as 'hippie ha-ole' compared to the ha-oles of La-haina who were sailors, surfers and beachcombers.

While walking the streets of Pa'ia today, you are still likely to see some hippie throwbacks with long unkempt hair and handmade draw string pants or shorts and shirts of contrasting fabrics and patterns with strands of beads dangling around their necks.

Today, however, instead of the hippie look, you are more likely to see the yuppie look as yuppie ha-oles stroll the streets of Pa'ia; the men wearing commercially made zippered pants or shorts with breezy shirts made on Bali while the women on their way to or from the beach, wear a hand dyed silk sarong over their two piece swimsuits.

You will also see a number of windsurfers from Europe cruising the streets of Pa'ia with their windsurfing rigs strapped to their car roof racks. European youths who have come to enjoy the waves off of Ho'okipa Beach just outside of Pa'ia who, along with the ever increasing numbers of tourist couples and tourist families, are continually wandering in an out of the restaurants, boutiques and antique stores. It is rare these days to see locals of Filipino or Oriental origin hanging out on the street corners of Pa'ia.

In fact, Pa'ia has become so busy that the traffic tie up at the Stop Sign where Baldwin Avenue and the Hana Highway meet has finally been transformed into a traffic light. Gone are the days when you could goof off driving around in circles at this intersection in the middle of the day.

As you walk the streets of Pa'ia, you will discover a couple of mom-and-pop family owned grocery stores, a couple of hair cutters, a dry cleaners, a video store and an ice cream parlor along with some classy little boutiques featuring the finest island fashions and island styles, plus art galleries, antique stores, restaurants and businesses catering to the surfers, windsurfers and beach goers.

OUTDOOR ADVENTURES

One place highly recommended for surf and sail board rentals in Pa'ia is **Hi-Tech**, Maui's oldest windsurf shop situated on Baldwin Avenue next to **Mana Foods.** Along with a fine selection of beach wear and accessories, Hi-Tech can shape boards, rent boards or even set you up with lessons if you're new to the sport. Call 579-9297 about rentals and lessons.

Another outrageous outdoor adventure that begins and ends in Pa'ia is **Cruiser Bob's** downhill bike ride from the summit of Hale-a-kala to the Hana Highway. Cruiser Bob is the originator of this biking activity. He vans you to the 10,023 foot summit, provides you with bike, helmet, rain slicker (if needed), gloves and a two man safety crew to lead the way. It's all downhill from then on. Down 38 curvey miles to

112 * THE NARROW WINDING ROAD

PA'IA - OUR FAVORITE PLACES

Pa'ia. My son and I took the ride, it was quite a thrilling trip. Call 579-8444 for schedules and to make reservations.

Cruiser Bob is also responsible for the bike lanes now extending from Lahaina through Pa'ia out to Ho'okipa Beach. His dream is to turn Maui into a biking mecca. He is also working along with the County and State in turning the old Maui Trail between Pa'ia and Ka-hu-lui into a linear park for walking and bicycling. Unfortunately the only real opposition to this goal is A&B Properties who would rather build structures on the land and make money.

BOUTIQUES

Julie Vandyke, whom I first met when she was living in Upper Na-hiku near Hana, now owns her own shop on Baldwin Avenue. Until recently it was called **The Northshore Silks & Body Shop** and is now simply **The Silk Gallery**. Here Julie displays her hand painted clothing along with some Bali imports and a selection of charming gift items. Besides her finished pieces available here and in La-haina, Julie can design one-of-a-kind originals for you on request. 579-9478.

A few doors up from **The Silk Gallery** is **Creative Culture**, one of Pa'ia's newest boutiques. Here you will find beautiful handcrafted clothing, accessories, jewelry and authentic treasures from Guatamala, Bali and many other exotic places around the world. **Creative Culture** has a façade as vibrant as the fabrics inside. This is one of those places that fits the description "a delight to the visual senses." 579-9984.

Think Good Thoughts is next on Baldwin Avenue. In this biggest little store every bit of space is filled with bright colors and gift items. The focus is T-Shirts with a positive message. Messages which inspire you to 'think good thoughts' about life, the environment and humanity. There are also tie dyes in electrifying color combinations, cotton sundresses, swimsuits and children's clothing along with Grateful Dead products, cards, journals and gift paper made from recycled materials. 579-8629.

Across the street is **Maui Girl & Co.**, which for many years was called, **The Clothes Addict**, one of the oldest shops in Pa'ia town. **Maui Girl**, features a wide variety of swimsuits and beachwear. What really makes this boutique special is its extensive collection of Aloha shirts from the 1930's. These shirts are called 'silkies.' Cyndi Lauper, Billy Joel, Christy Brinkley, Ringo Starr and other celebrities have come in looking for these one-of-a-kind collector items which are often framed once they become too fragile to wear. 579-9266.

Further up Baldwin Avenue on the same side of the street as **Maui Girls**, across from the Post Office and Pa'ia's only bank, in one of Pa'ia's many classic old buildings, is the **'Ukulele Clothing Company** which specializes in casual attire for the "aloha lifestyle." An exciting array of prints are designed and hand screen-printed in Ha-'iku at **'Ukulele's** own innovative textile printing factory. **'Ukulele** quality is very good and their selections are broad and original. The island feeling permeates this store. 579-9960.

Coming back to the Hana Highway is another of our favorite places to shop. **Boutique II** situated on the mau-ka (mountain) side of the street as you enter Pa'ia. Owners Patty and Dyan

PA'IA: OUR FAVORITE PLACES

design many of the fashions (all made from natural fabrics). They also personally design their shoe selection. Especially noteworthy are the hand dyed silk sarongs, or pareaus, which can be tied many different ways making them suitable for beach or for evening wear. 579-8602.

The only place in Pa'ia to buy your kids or grandkids aloha shirts, shorts or tiny muu muus along with women's resort wear is **Just You & Me Kid**. All styles are designed and manufactured on Maui by Creations by Carol Ann. It is located next to the **Hana Hou Art Gallery** on the right side of the street as you enter Pa'ia town. **Just You & Me Kid** also has a new outlet at the Marriott Hotel in Ka-anapali resort. 579-9433.

As you come back to the beginning of Pa'ia Town is **Nuage Bleu** another great little shop with an exciting selection of clothing, fashion accessories and interesting gift items. Owned by Michele and Teri, two world travelers, who, on their journeys to different parts of the world, continually search for the fresh and the innovative. Consequently, **Nuage Bleu** reflects a synthesis of international flair with island style sophistication. 579-9792.

Pa'ia has something unique for everyone. If hats are your thing, **Paradise Millinery** is the place to go. Located on the ocean side as you enter Pa'ia, **Paradise Millinery** features original hats and accessories designed to suit your needs and personality. All custom orders are exclusively made by Katherine Carey. 243-2HAT.

ARTS, CRAFTS & ANTIQUES

The **Maui Crafts Guild** is one of the oldest galleries in Pa'ia. It is the first store on the left as you enter Pa'ia after passing Baldwin Beach Park. The **Maui Crafts Guild** is co-operatively owned by 40 local craftspeople of outstanding ability. Here you will find baskets from island plants, local wood bowls and boxes, ceramics, bamboo, jewelry, etchings, glass, wearable art and more can be found in this unique store where the prices are practically wholesale and your salesperson is one of the artisans. Many of Maui's best known artists and craftspeople were seen here first. 579-9697.

Across the street, next to **Just You & Me Kid**, is the **Hana Hou Art Gallery & Gift Shop** which along with the great art featuring local Maui artists also carries one-of-a-kind heirloom jewelry, fresh water pearls, petroglyph art and wonderful gifts made from exotic island woods like mango, monkey pod and rosewood. 579-8185.

Next to **Summerhouse**, another of Pa'ia's oldest boutiques, on the ocean side of the Hana Highway as you enter Pa'ia, is a tiny shop called **Oh Deybra!** Deybra is a popular Maui favorite whose paintings present a whimsical view of island life and island images.

Wandering into the **Maui Crafts Guild**, **Hana Hou**, **Oh, Deybra!** and the **Maui Sculpture Gallery** (corner of Baldwin Ave. and the Hana Highway) to look at the art pieces is equivalent to walking through a small museum where you can stop to look at each piece and marvel at the beauty of design and skill of execution.

Adding to the museum like quality of Pa'ia is the fascinating Hawaiian artifacts found at another of Pa'ia's

PA'IA: OUR FAVORITE PLACES

older establishments, the **Pa'ia Trading Company** which is located just before Baldwin Avenue on the Hana Highway. All the antiques were gathered on Maui from antique furniture to useful and unusual collectibles like scrimshaw knives, glass bottles and silk kimonos. 579-9472.

Upcountry Maui Antiques is another favorite place for antique hunters living on the island or visiting. It is situated on the ocean side of the Hana Highway just after the **Maui Crafts Guild** and is located in an old garage giving it plenty of room for a wide selection of antique furniture. You will also find brass oil lamps, Matson Menu Covers, dolls, tea pots, vintage radios, clocks, jewelry and interesting bric bracs not found elsewhere. 579-9707.

RESTAURANTS

Depending on the time of day, there are different eateries that my family and I prefer. If we arrive in Pa'ia early enough for breakfast, **Charley's** is the place to go.

Offering a variety of omelettes at reasonable prices, in addition to pancakes, waffles and various side orders. Service is always courteous and it's a good place to run into friends whom I haven't seen in awhile.

Likewise, on the way home to Hana after a day of shopping for supplies and doing chores, **Charley's** is a good place to have dinner. I usually prefer one of their fresh fish dinners, my wife loves their gorgonzola cheese dressing on her salad with a glass of wine and my son likes the Portuguese sausage on spaghetti. Occasionally we'll indulge in dessert and enjoy one of the best mud pies on the island.

It should also be mentioned that **Charley's** Vegetarian and Tex-Mex pizzas were judged best at the First Annual Island Wide Pizza Wars.

The owners of **Charley's** now have plans to open a world class dinner house fronting Pa'ia Bay to be called **Pa'ia Bay**. The design is based on a picture found at the Maui Historical Society of a vintage 1930's establishment. **Charley's** is located at the far end of town on the mau-ka side of the Hana Highway. 579-9453.

Yet another favorite place for lunch or dinner and another very comfortable and pleasant place to sit, relax and 'talk story' is **Vegan's**.

As the name implies, **Vegan's** is strictly vegetarian. That's vegetarian without any animal products meaning no eggs or milk. **Vegan's** restaurant was begun by a commune of individuals dedicated to living a vegan life-style.

The healthful food at **Vegan's** is always great for fruit smoothees, home made soups, desserts and full dinner platters. The new owners of **Vegan's** have added some excellent Thai food dishes to the menu. **Vegan's** is a small, friendly restaurant located up Baldwin Avenue on the left side of the street past the main cluster of shops. There are tables and chairs outside on the sidewalk to accommodate the **Vegan's** ever increasing popularity. 579-9144.

Just down from **Vegan's**, is a strange assortment of businesses squeezed into one small old building. There is a shop run by a Christian youth mission, **The Pa'ia Bike Shop**, **The Pa'ia Snack Shop** and **Papaya**

PA'IA: OUR FAVORITE PLACES

John's. The **Snack Shop** offers shave ice and plate lunch specials which are tasty and inexpensive. Young locals and surfers are constantly in and out.

Papaya John's is a place you have to visit. Here you will find papaya products based on formulas originated by the late Dr. Kurt Koesel in the 1930's when he used papaya to cure himself of an illness he got in the Caribbean.

Coming to Maui in the 60's, Dr. Koesel developed many tasty preparation which maximized the healthful benefits of his energy bars. These products, made from specially cultivated fruit averaging 15 pounds each, are rich in enzymes and are noted for their ability to assist nutrient assimilation and to relieve digestive disorders.

I once spent three days hiking in Hale-a-kala Crater eating only the morning, afternoon and dinner bars. The morning bar is a cleansing combination, while the lunch bar is the most like candy and the evening bar is highest in vitamins and protein. Dr. Koesel died in 1990, a week before his 90th birthday. Everyone on Maui missed these wonderful products and now, thanks to **Papaya John's** dedication, they are back. 579-9608.

Other favorite spots which satisfy other preferences include **Peach's & Crumble**, another great place just off the corner of where Baldwin Avenue meets the Hana Highway. **Peach's & Crumble** makes excellent sandwiches and offers the widest selection of desserts and munchies. Sweet, yummy munchies. They also have coffee beans and a grinder for fresh ground blends like chocolate macadamian, banana-nut, peaches 'n' cream and of course the ever popular Kona blends.

Though **Peach's & Crumble** has two counters and a few stools, it is a favorite hangout for the early morning coffee drinkers who instead of an omelette prefer a fresh baked pastry, muffin, breakfast biscuit or scone. 579-8612.

Still further up Baldwin Avenue and on the same side of the street as **Peach's & Crumble** is **Picnics**.

Picnics has a great breakfast, lunch and early dinner menu. All at reasonable prices. Besides catering to the early morning coffee drinking crowd, **Picnics** has specialties like yogurt shakes, fresh-baked bakery items along with a wide variety of fresh made sandwiches including fish burgers, great tasting spinach nut burgers, tofu burgers and the All-American favorite, hamburgers. **Picnics** hamburgers are made with organic beef raised up the Hana Highway in Ha-'iku. Even my teenage son can tell the difference. 579-8021.

Both **Picnics** and **Peach's & Crumble** also cater to the tourists who are heading out to Hana, and possibly beyond, by preparing box lunches to go.

Across the street from **Picnics** is the only bank in town, the Post Office and one of the best health food stores on the island, **Mana Foods.** A wide variety of products and great looking produce grown without pesticides or chemical fertilizers. The organic produce here is often as inexpensive as the pesticide sprayed produce shipped in from the Mainland and sold at the larger supermarkets. Though it should be pointed out that more and more of the large chain supermarkets are now

PA'IA: OUR FAVORITE PLACES

carrying organically grown produce as well as a selection of health food items. It's good to see these changes.

Mana Foods is also the place to go for great vegetarian take-out items, fresh baked bread, cold drinks, juices, chips, ice cream, munchies and bottled water. And now **Mana** has added a Salad Bar. **Mana Foods** is usually my last stop before heading home to Hana after a long day of shopping and chores on what those of us who live in Hana call, the Other Side. Mana is the Hawaiian word for 'power.' 579-8078.

Then there is the new **Wunderbar** and **Caffe Paradiso** restaurants with their casual cosmopolitan atmospheres.

Caffe Paradiso is situated on the Hana Highway next to **Charley's**. The two owners of the **Paradiso**, Michele and Paolo, serve Mediterreanean cuisine from Italy, Spain, France and Greece prepared by Chef Paolo Bucchioni. **Paradiso's** has a lovely outside garden area in addition to its intimate indoor setting. Beside lunch and dinner, pastries and espresso are available in the mornings. 579-8819.

The **Wunderbar - Cafe, Restaurant, Bar** is on the ma-kai (ocean) side of the Hana Highway as you enter town after the **Maui Crafts Guild**. **Wunderbar** is another new edition presenting an international flair with excellent food preparations of steak, pork and veal plus many vegetarian selections. Since **Wunderbar** opened it's doors, this place has been busy for breakfast, lunch and dinner. **Wunderbar** also has room enough for live bands and musicians making this Pa'ia's hottest evening night spot. 579-8808.

Of course any listing of Hana Highway eateries would not be complete without mention of the now historical landmark, **Mama's Fish House**. **Mama's** is located a few miles outside of Pa'ia in an area called Ku'au.

Mama's Fish House has become one of the most acclaimed world class dining establishments on Maui. Its reputation is international as a place to enjoy an outstanding sunset along with fine wines and fine food.

Years ago a fresh fish dinner at **Mama's** was a treat that always felt like a celebration. Even now eating at **Mama's** continually adds to my delusion that I have died and went to Heaven.

When I first arrived on Maui, the restaurant was rarely crowded as the Hana Highway past Pa'ia was rarely traveled by tourists. So it was fairly easy to get a window seat and watch the changing colors of the sky as the sun went down. What made **Mama's** one of the best restaurants on Maui was Mama herself. She was the cook and even today, the memory of her *poisson cru* makes my mouth water. Eventually, Mama sold the restaurant.

But the tradition goes on. Every appertizer, every entree is a memory. The curried fish in particular is outstanding and the dish I have most frequently.

The atmosphere at **Mama's** has always been friendly and a perfect example of the alo-ha spirit and island style. No experience of the drive to Hana and back can be considered complete with out stopping at least once for an exquisite fish dinner and Maui sunset at **Mama's Fish House**. 579-8488.

Ka-hului: Back To The Beginning

The beginning of the Hana Highway used to be lined with new car and used car lots, car rentals, furniture and lighting fixture stores, tire repair shops and industrial outlets for propane, electrical supplies, etc. In recent years things have been changing. Now, on either side of the wide, coconut tree lined meridian, you will find new services and restaurants to accommodate the growing needs of Maui's growing population.

In addition to the many new shops at this end of the Hana Highway, there are also many shops along Alamaha Street. Alamaha Street is parallel to the Hana Highway, extending from Dairy Road to not quite as far as Ka-ahumanu Boulevard. Along Alamaha Street you will find a lumber yard, hardware store, futon outlet, printers, the Hi-Fi Hospital and Wild Bill's American Motorcycles. This is the edge of the area called the Ka-hului Industrial Park. Like most of Ka-hului, the land here is owned by Alexander and Baldwin and was formerly part of their sugar plantation.

RESTAURANTS

On Alamaha Street among the beer distributors, paint stores and other windowless warehouses with roll-up bay doors, a half a mile down the street from Dairy Road at 162 Alamaha, you will find another of Maui's best places to eat, **Ming Yuen**.

Ming Yuen Chinese Restaurant is one of our favorite places. Even before you walk in, you are engulfed by wonderful aromas that make you smile with anticipation. **Ming Yuen** was voted by the residents of Maui as the Best Chinese Restaurant. They do a consistently great job preparing authentic Cantonese and Szechuanese cuisine at moderate prices. Try their Hot Sour Soup, Mu Shu Pork, Sweet Sour Shrimps, Szechuan Spicy Eggplant, Lemon Chicken and House Special Noodles. They have some fabulous vegetarian food too. Open for lunch and dinner. For reservations call their friendly staff at 871-7787.

SERVICES

Homegrown Island Arts is a real special place to visit for affectionatos of Hawaii and Hawaiiana. It is the only gift shop in this area offering a quality selection of wood carvings, handcrafted bowls, baskets, earrings and jewelry, paintings and prints by local artists, plus photo and art books. **Homegrown Island Arts** is situated on the corner of Dairy Road and Alamaha. 877-0399.

Before or after lunch, you may want to drive over to **Planetsaviors** now located at 444 Hana Highway. **Planetsaviors** is "an earth friendly department store" and is the only establishment on Maui featuring a complete line of environmentally supportive products for home, garden and automotive needs. Along with the energy efficient light bulbs, ecologically safe detergents, there is clothing made from unbleached cotton and some fabric made from hemp. There are also many unusual and useful gifts items.

In Hana, the house I live in is powered by solar panels so the 13 watt flourescent bulbs are a great energy saver compared to the equivalent 75 watt incandescent bulbs more commonly available. Likewise, much of our sink and shower water flows into our garden and so it is comforting to know that the products we get from **Planetsaviors** are not harmful for the earth or for my family. Every time I go in to **Planetsav-**

iors I invariably find something special to give to someone I love from a wooden toy for my child or a hanging planter to give to a friend. 871-1561.

GNC - General Nutrition Center, another business located on the corner of Dairy Road at 444 Hana Highway, is a nationally known franchise providing quality food supplementation. In addition to all the top brands of vitamins, minerals, juices and healthful snacks, **GNC** also has a wide variety of supplements used by body builders, exercise enthusiasts and anyone who desires to maintain good health and well-being. At **GNC** you will find the sales help very knowledgeable in assisting you. 877-5222.

Maui East-West Clinic is located above **Planetsaviors** and **GNC** on the corner of the Hana Highway and Dairy Road is the place to go for acupuncture, chiropractic adjustments and naturopathic preparations. Dr. Kevin Davison has developed a reputation for his ability to deal with trauma due to sports injuries, auto and job related accidents. His greater renown is in his ability to assist his patients to achieve optimum health through an integrated program of nutrition, herbalism, homeopathy, physical manipulation, counseling and oriental medicine to treat as well as prevent disease. 871-4722.

Class Act Tattoo Shop is also located above **Planetsaviors** and **GNC** at 444 Hana Highway. Samantha and Dave carry on the age old tradition of body tattooing. Tattooing was once the primary form of body decoration in Hawaii, throughout Polynesia and in many other parts of the world, and in recent years body tattooing has again become fashionably acceptable. 871-7464.

444 Hair is located at the other end of 444 Hana Highway and is the place for good looking cuts by outstanding stylists. **444 Hair** is a full service salon providing facials, waxing, skin care specialist, licensed therapeutic massage therapists and knowledgeable practitioners of Aromatherapy. Aromatherapy utilizes the essential oils of aromatic plants in special formulations to relax and refresh your body, mind and spirit. **444 Hair** has a second location in Kihei at the Gateway Plaza. 871-8444 or in Kihei, 875-8444.

Oasis Maui Garden Supply Center, located at 230 Hana Highway, has been assisting Maui gardeners and farmers get the best result since 1977. **Oasis Maui** is the most comprehensive supplier of botanical insecticides, organic seeds, organic soil additives and gardening books for all levels from beginner to large scale farmer. 871-2634.

OUTDOOR ADVENTURES

Hi-Tech Surf Sports is Maui's oldest windsurf shop with its original location in Pa'ia on Baldwin Avenue adjacent to **Mana Foods**. **Hi-Tech** in Kahului in addition to sales and rentals of their high quality handcrafted boards also sells beach wear, surfing gear and other beach and sea sport accessories. Call 877-2111 about rentals or lessons.

Hunt Hawaii Surf & Sail run by Doug and Tawney Hunt used to be located in Pa'ia on the Hana Highway and is now located off the Hana Highway on the road to the Ka-hu-lui Airport. Doug Hunt has the distinction of being the first windsurfer to do a "loop" in the air and keep sailing. Doug also hand shapes custom surf and sailboards at the Hunt Hawaii factory in Ha-'iku. 871-1240.

OTHER WONDERFUL MAUI THINGS TO DO

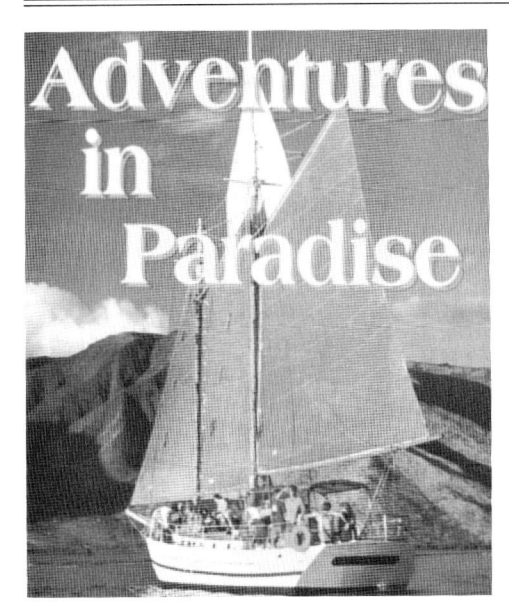

MAUI CLASSIC CHARTERS

LONG'S CENTER, KIHEI 96753
(808) 879-8188

What a fun time we had sailing from Ma-'alaea Harbor to Molokini Island, spending the day in gentle Pacific waters aboard the 54 foot catamaran Four Winds. Even as residents of Maui, we felt we were on vacation. As they say in their advertising, "...passengers are always smiling when they sail in to the harbor...."

The friendly crew took good care of everyone on board. They prepared a continental breakfast and bar-be-que lunch and made sure everyone had fins and masks and knew how to use them. The two meals, snorkel gear, fishing tackle for Hawaiian game fishing and unlimited beer, wine and soda were all included in the price of the cruise.

Jaimie was the specialist on board available to introduce us to the excitement of SNUBA diving. In SNUBA a tank floats on the surface to which you are connected by a long hose. This gives you the mobility and comfort to explore the sea without the equipment, diving ability or training of scuba or the need for a lengthy certification course.

There is also a video professional who films the complete excursion. What a great way to bring home memories while you're on board meeting people from around the world, sliding down the on-board water slide, kicked back soaking up the rays, and when your beneath the sea surrounded by the many varieties of tropical fish which makes Molokini reef one of the best places to swim, snorkel and dive.

For non-swimmers, older folks and kids, the Four Winds has large submarine style glassbottom windows which provide a close-up view of the exotic fish which are attracted to this area. You will also see members of your own family as they snorkel by exploring the the world beneath the sea.

During Whale Watching season (December - May) the Four Winds is the only boat that provides a Greenpeace naturalist to inform you while you listen to the song of the humpbacks on the ships hydrophone as these giants of the sea make their annual visit to the warm birthing waters of the Hawaiian islands. A percentage of each ticket is given to Greenpeace Hawaii in their effort to save the whales and preserve Maui's marine environment.

OTHER WONDERFUL MAUI THINGS TO DO

CLUB LANAI
Your Private Beach Resort.
KAHALEPOLAOA • LANA'I
(808) 871-1144
MAINLAND TOLL FREE 1-800-531-5262

I've lived on Maui since 1974 and I've never been to Lana'i. It was all pineapple plantation and nothing to do. But since 1984, eight acres, including 13 miles of untouched white sand beach, have been developed into what is now referred to as "Hawaii's Private Playground in the Sun." And rightly so.

To enjoy the full day activities of Club Lana'i, my family and I departed Lahaina Harbor at 8am aboard one of their luxury catamarans for a beautiful 45 minute cruise nine miles across the channel. It seems Lahaina always has clear skys, calm waters and rainbows in the West Maui Mountains.

The Club Lanai motto is "Do It All or Do Nothing At All." And in order to satisfy this motto, everything is available including all you can eat and all you can drink.

We started with snorkeling off the Club Lana'i boat at Turtle Reef, one of the largest living reefs where many varieties of reef fish can be observed.

After showering off, we took a wagon ride past an ancient temple (heiau) to the historic church of the old plantation town. We learned alot about the life and culture of the islands. After the wagon ride, we took a stroll around the facility which revealed something interesting around every corner. There was an Hawaiian village, an artistian's cove with demonstrations of old Hawaiian crafts, and all kinds of activities to get involved in such as badminton, volleyball and croquet. A favorite for our two year old was the marine touch tanks and its exhibit of reef fish.

Lunch was tasty with plenty to eat and a great way to meet some of our fellow escapees from civilization. During lunch there was a hula presentation with all the kids participating and everyone laughing and having lots of fun.

Before departure back to Maui at 2:30, we had plenty of time to enjoy kayaking, bike riding off the property down a country road followed by a stroll along one of the five mile stretches of beach where we played in the sand before finally surrendering to the hammocks swaying in the breeze. Couldn't have been a more perfect day. We were sorry to have to leave as this was definitely the Hawaiiana life style of choice.

At 3:30, after a pleasant sail back to Lahaina Harbor, the crew immediately began preparing their vessel for its daily sunset cocktail cruise.

THE NARROW WINDING ROAD

OTHER WONDERFUL MAUI THINGS TO DO

THE HAWAII EXPERIENCE DOMED THEATER

824 Front St., Lahaina * For Information: 661-8314
Continuous Showings 10am to 10pm Daily

One of the reasons for this section of the book was to share with you some of the best of Maui. And this movie is incredible. The impact is staggering. Superlatives come easy. Incredible! Spectacular! Fantastic! From the very first moment to the last, the viewer is riveted to the screen by the splendor and intensity of images. Everyone who lives on or who visits Maui must see this movie. It's more than worth the price of admission.

The movie's title is "Hawaii: Islands of the Gods." It begins with an eruption of a volcano and sweeps you along with glimpses of Hawaiian history, arts and island topography. The fauna, flora and undersea beauty of Hawaii is all here.

What makes this the most outstanding movie on Maui is the 180° giant domed screen which is over three stories high (35 feet). This million dollar production took three years to produce and is truly a work of art.

ALEX AIR

(808) 871-0792
MAINLAND TOLL FREE 800-462-2281

Like every activity I recommend, this is one every resident of Maui should do at least once and should be at the top of the Must-Do list of every visitor. Unlike some of the activities mentioned, this one is an exciting thrill ride. I highly recommend you schedule this one after you see the movie at the Dome Theater and before you enjoy a leisurely cruise and a day of play and relaxation at Club Lana'i.

In researching helicopter tours, I chose ALEXAIR because the Hughes 500 is the smallest with less passengers, guaranteeing everyone a window seat with couples sitting together. Being smaller, it maneuvers easier and gets right into every place imaginable. If you love the beauty of Maui from the ground, wait till you see it from the air. Whether you are a visitor or resident, a grown up or a kid, a helicopter ride along the Hana Coast or the Sunset Special will be another Maui experience you won't ever forget. Truly awesome.

OTHER WONDERFUL MAUI THINGS TO DO

Old Lahaina Luau

505 FRONT STREET, LAHAINA

667-1998

With so many new activities in Lahaina, I asked those in the know; and all unanimously agreed, the Old Lahaina Lu'au is the best Lu'au by far which must be why they were given the prestigious Five Kahili Award in the Hawai'i Visitors Bureau "Keep it Hawaii" program.

From the moment you enter the Lu'au grounds, you are engulfed by the festive mood. With all you can eat and drink it's no wonder everyone has a good time. The feast begins with the unearthing of the Kalua roast pig from the imu (traditonal Hawaiian underground oven). The buffet selection is fabulous. There's the sweet tasting pig, grilled sirloin, pineapple chicken, baked mahi mahi, sweet potato from Hana, lomi lomi salmon, poki ahi, steamed taro leaves, local style chicken long rice, haupia, banana bread, salad, fresh fruits and plenty of poi to mix in with the other great tastes.

Though there is music and singing during dinner as the sun is setting, the main show begins after sunset. The performers tell the history of Hawai'i from early migration across the Pacific Ocean to modern times. The story is told through powerful chants, original instruments and mesmerizing hula. Whenever we have visitors from the Mainland, we treat them with an evening at the Old Lahaina Lu'au.

AVALON

844 FRONT STREET, LAHAINA

667-5559

There are a few restaurants in Lahaina who have built their reputation on good food, comfortable environment and an outstanding chef. Chef Mark Ellman is, as others have said, the "Merlin of Avalon." His presence permeates. Sometimes appearing as the gracious host and always as the creative genius of food combinations that make one's taste buds ecstatic and compulse the unihibited to lick their plate.

Every thing on the menu sounds phenomenal with enough variety that you can eat at Avalon every night and swoon with delight. How about Hawaiian ahi tostada with feta cheese and white bean salad. Or, Chicken marinated in palm sugar, grilled and served with Balinese peanut sauce. Or, one of Mark Ellman's signature dishes, Chili seared salmon layered with potatoes, eggplant, greens, mango and tomato salsa with a plum vinaigrette. I love that one. And how about grilled fish with garlic black bean sauce. The list goes on. You have no choice but to come back many times. Ending each meal of course with the unique Caramel Miranda: macadamia nut ice cream surrounded by exotic fruits bathed in a delicate flavored caramel sauce. Yum!

CHEF / OWNER MARK ELLMAN

OTHER WONDERFUL THINGS TO DO

Longhi's

MAUI'S MOST POPULAR RESTAURANT — 1993 Peoples Choice Award

888 FRONT STREET - LAHAINA
667-2288

Bob Longhi came to Maui, found very few places offering quality food, took a chance and, in 1976, opened his own fine food establishment. He advertised it as "...a restaurant created by a man who loves to eat." Using his own receipes, he provided quality breakfasts, lunches and dinners. The menu at Longhi's is always changing and because it is always changing, it isn't written down. Instead, the waiter, or waitress, pulls up a chair and tells you what's cooking. Divided into categories and with everything a la carte, you mix and match and then voila, it all falls into place. You get lots of great tastes and flavors and another fabulous meal at Longhi's. Great salads, pastas, seafoods and steaks all complemented by an award winning wine list.

When Bob first opened Longhi's, the restaurant only occupied the street level. As his reputation grew, so did the lines of visitors and island residents waiting hungrily outside. As soon as the upstairs became available, Longhi's expanded and more than doubled the space. The upstairs also includes a bandstand and dance floor. Over the years, we used to pack in to hear George Benson on guitar or some musicians playing jazz or someone singing ballads. With expansion upstairs, there's plenty of room to have a really good time dancing to local bands and visiting musicians.

Chez Paul

RESTAURANT ✦ FRANÇAIS

OLOWALU VILLAGE - LAHAINA
661-3843

Since 1968, Chez Paul, Hawaii's oldest French Restaurant, consistently pleases. It is comfortable, pleasant, intimate and elegant. The service is impeccable. Every detail of this restaurant is tastefully done to conjure up the atmosphere of a French country inn.

I especially like restaurants where the menu is exciting to read and Chez Paul's menu is especially fun. Fond d'artichaud a la framboise. Feuillete aux champignons sauvages. Waterzooi de homard au Champagne. Etcetera. Of course under each title is a mouth watering description in English.

When there are so many appetizers that taste as good as they do at Chez Paul, my wife and I like to order "family style" - several appetizers and at least one entree. In this way we share everything and taste everything. Ordering "family style" provides plenty of surprises and smiles of delight. Food prepared as exquisitely as it is at Chez Paul renders the most articulate individual speechless. M-m-m, m-m-m, oh-h-h, ah. Fortunately, the fresh baked baquettes make it easy to wipe each plate clean by soaking up the lobster sauce, the champagne, shallots, cream and capers, or the juices of the poisson et homard in sorrel sauce. And don't forget to save room for an incredible dessert: profiterralles au chocolate.

OTHER WONDERFUL MAUI THINGS TO DO

Carelli's ON THE BEACH

2980 S. KIHEI ROAD - KIHEI
875-0001

Outstanding food and an outstanding location. As the sun goes down, the stars come out. Located near Wailea on beautiful Keawakapu Beach, Carelli's reputation for a classic Italian setting, fine dining, casual elegance and friendly atmosphere, keeps this a very busy place. Owners Tony Habib and Craig Delaney's inspiration for the menu and the style of service is Habib's late grandfather, Rocco Carelli and the family tradition: "you are invited to our home for supper."

Seating is first come, first serve; but even if you have to wait for a table, there's a friendly bar and a great Mangia Menu with a wide variety of tasty appetizers. Although dinner is only served from 6:00 p.m. until 10 p.m., Carelli's Mangia Bar with cocktails is open until 11:00 p.m. The Mangia Bar is sort of a restaurant within a restaurant and seemed like a great place to enjoy good food and meet people.

The seasonal menu changes every three months and always features a wide array of wonderfully prepared fresh fish (Pesce Del Giorno) and Italian masterpieces like Connie's Ceasar Salad, Ravioli Spinaci, Rigatoni Alla Napoletani, Linguine Con Vongole, Costolette Di Agnello Alla Griglia and wood-fired pizza magnifico. And for dessert, what else but cappuccino and Tiramisu.

Lobster Cove

WAILEA IKI, WAILEA
879-7677

Dipping succulent lobster in the Lobster Cove's spicy sauce has got to be an all time great experience. Eating seared ahi sashimi on a bed of shiitake mushrooms has got to be another of the all time great experiences. Eating anything on the Lobster Cove menu is an outstanding experience. The Peppered Crust Salmon is delectable. As is the Thailand Style Mahi Mahi. As is the fresh island fish prepared in Special Beurre Blanc Lobster Cove.

Or you can order an appetizer from Harry's Sushi Bar, a corner of the Lobster Cove which seems to have a life of its own. Plenty of sake, sushi, smiling faces and friendly conversation.

Besides the live lobster dish there are Lobster Cakes, Lobster Bisque and Feuilette (diced lobster in a puffed pastry shell). Other shell fish available are dungeness crab, clams, scallops, shrimp and oyster combinations. For meat eaters, there's Filet Mignon with a cognac flambee, cream and green pepper corn. The Lobster Cove's outrageous dessert is the Sin-Bad Pineapple - marinated slices of pineapple lightly fried, topped with mac nut ice cream covered in hot Belgian chocolate sauce. The sauces and food are so good that the Lobster Cove is another 'lick your plate' kind of restaurant.

OTHER WONDERFUL MAUI THINGS TO DO

Casanova Italian Restaurant & Deli
1166 MAKAWAO AVENUE - MAKAWAO
572-0220

Casanova has many faces and appeals to different facets of the community. For breakfast and lunch, there's the Deli offering pastas, sandwiches, desserts and fresh brewed coffee, tea, espresso or cappuccino. The Deli has long been a favorite place for upcountry residents to hang out and watch the people and cars go by on Makawao Avenue.

As the Deli closes, the Restaurant opens for fine dining at its best. The upcountry atmosphere is always warm and intimate. There's casual seating adjacent the bar for those who just want antipasto, salad or a pizza from the wood-fired oven. For the serious diner there's great pastas, fresh fish and meat entrees along with the specials of the day. The motto at Casanova is "Real Italian Food From Real Italians." No wonder in both 1992 and 1993, Casanova's reputation for excellence has resulted in the Maui News' reader survey declaring Casanova "the best Italian restaurant on Maui."

After dinner, Casanova again transforms. Top performers from all over the country will get your feet moving on one of Maui's largest dance floors. Live bands range from rock, raggae, country to cajun. There have also been special dinner shows with music legends like Taj Mahal, Willie Nelson or Los Lobos. Morning till night, Casanova is the place to be.

Hali'imaile General Store Maui
900 HALI'IMAILE ROAD, HALI'IMAILE
572-2666

Located upcountry on the slopes of Hale-a-kala, the Hali'imaile General Store was built in 1929 in the midst of a 1,000-acre pineapple plantation. The General Store has been beautifully refurbished by owners Joe and Bev Gannon and now serves lunch and dinner seven days a week as well as Sunday brunch.

Since its opening in 1988, the Hali'imaile General Store has become one of Maui's most popular places to eat. Thanks to Chef Bev Gannon's creative approach to cuisine, the menu is full of memorable combinations and innovative surprises. Using the freshest of ingredients from Maui's local agricultural community, fresh fish and the finest cuts of meats, diners at Hali'imaile General Store are guaranteed to satisfy.

The menu influences range from Mediterreanean to Southeast Asia. The appetizers and salads alone can keep you busy all evening. There's Bev's renown crab dip served on a 6" Boboli, the Brie & Grape Quesadilla or Peking Duck Salad. The entrees are, as the menu states, "amazing." I love the Szechuan Barbecued Salmon and Coconut Seafood Curry. If I'm really hungry, I go for the Filet Mignon or Rack of Lamb Hunan Style. There's also an excellent selection of wines and great desserts. Nothing is usual and everything is superb.

126 * THE NARROW WINDING ROAD

OTHER WONDERFUL MAUI THINGS TO DO

KPOA
FM 93.5 Lahaina - FM 107.3 Wailuku

"Maui's ALOHA Station"

Maui radio station KPOA, heard on Maui, Lana'i, Moloka'i, portions of the Big Island, O'ahu and cable T.V., is the only true Hawaiian station broadcasting from Maui. From 1 a.m. to 8 p.m. the varied sounds of Hawai'i can be heard on FM 93.5 in Lahaina and FM 107.3 Wailuku, Kahului and Upcountry.

For many people living on the Mainland, Hawaiian music seems to be limited to hapa-haole like Pearly Shells or Lovely Hula Hands accompanied by someone plucking notes on an 'ukulele. It is only when those same individuals come to the islands that they are exposed to the rich musical heritage that is Hawai'i. There is no better place to experience those tunes than on KPOA.

TRADITIONAL HAWAIIAN

In this category can be included the great chants of olden times. Powerful chants accompanied by the ipu (gourd) or the 'ohe hano 'ihu (nose flute). One of my favorites is an album called, Pele by Hula Master Keli'i Tau'a. These are chants to Pele, the Volcano Goddess.

Also in this category are sounds from more recent eras including traditional slack key greats like Gabby Pahinui, Eddie Kama'e and Peter Moon. Or the classic Rabbit Island Music Festival.

Though Gabby is my favorite, the songs of Auntie Edith Kanaka'ole and Auntie Alice Ku'uleialohapoina'ole transport me to another world. Their voices go deep into the soul one moment and then become as soft as a young girls.

More familiar sounds come under the title Chlangalang: Hulas for Lu'aus or Hawaiian Love Songs by Palani Vaughan, or any album by Auntie Genoa Keawe or Loyal Garner (voted Female Vocalist of 1992).

CONTEMPORARY HAWAIIAN

The most popular contemporary performers are the Cazimero Brothers, Kalapana, Brother Nolan and Cecilio & Kapono, the Beamer brothers. However, a duo named Hapa, featuring a musician from New York City named Barry Flanagan and a musician from O'ahu named Kelii Kaneali'i, is the group the KPOA DJ's predicts will be voted 1993 Album of the Year.

The 1992 Album of the Year is the Hawaiian Style Band, Male Vocalist is Del Beazley while the Best Group is the ever popular Makaha Sons of Ni'ihau. Also frequently heard everywhere is Pekelo, a Hana boy with a great album and the country-western style hit song, "Going Home to Hana, Maui."

JAWAIIAN REGGAE

This new category combines Jamaican rhythms with Hawaiian melodies. Most popular in this category is Willie K., Kapena and the most reggae sound of all, Ho'aikane, as heard on their new album, Kailua Kona.

To order a catalogue of these and other outstanding music selections, call or write the station store:

KPOA MUSIC & GIFT SHOP
505 Front Street
Lahaina, Hawai'i 96761
(808) 661-5599

THE NARROW WINDING ROAD *